The LOSER'S GUIDE to PERSONAL FAILURE

At Least 100 Secrets That Will Guarantee Self-Destruction

by Dean Christopher

From Magic Lamp Press
Venice, California

Magic Lamp

Press ™

www.AGuideToFailure.com

Cover design and photography by
Dave Newman Advertising
Burbank, CA
www.davenewman.com

The LOSER'S GUIDE to PERSONAL FAILURE

At Least 100 Secrets That Will Guarantee Self-Destruction

ISBN 1-882629-93-0

www.AGuideToFailure.com

CONTENTS

DEDICATION

AUTHOR'S DISCLAIMER

PREFACE

HOW TO USE THIS BOOK

INTRODUCTION
- FAILURE - Not What It's Cracked Up to Be
- Spotlight on Failure
- The Truth Will Help You Fail

Chapters

1: GENERIC FAILURE
- Failure is an Equal Opportunity Process
- Failure is a Many-Faceted Jewel
  - Case History

2: FAILURE AT LOVE AND SEX
- Love – Fraud or Delusion?
- Strategic Approaches to Failure at Love/Sex
- Failure Through Power Repulsiveness
- Body Weight and Physical Repulsion
- Height, Length and Physical Repulsion
- General Appearance and Physical Repulsion
- Hygiene, "Low-Giene" and Physical Repulsion
- Be Dirty !
- Putting Theory Into Practice
- Wardrobe, Grooming and Physical Repulsiveness

Dress Badly
Dirty, Tattered Clothes and Repulsion
Bold New Dimensions in Tastelessness
Failing At Financial Solvency = Failing At Love/Sex
Time Off For Bad Behavior
Anti-Etiquette Is the New Etiquette
Failure at the Dinner Table
Failure Through Visiting
Bereavements
Weddings
Other Religious Occasions
Sample Opening Lines to Hasten Failure at Love/Sex

3: FAILURE IN BUSINESS AND FINANCE
The Throbbing Heart of Investing: Investors
Business School
Getting Real with Real Estate
Failure Through Business Bloopers:
Making the Ooops! Factor Work For You
Money: The Engine of Finance
Buy High, Sell Low !
Failure Through Bold, Suicidal Enterpreneurism

3.5 FAILURE IN RADIO AND TELEVISION

4: FAILURE IN THE ARTS
About Acting
Actors: It's Never Too Early to Fail
Failing Your Casting Call
Sample Casting Call Rejection Inducers
Failure at Humor

Good News for Losers
Choosing a Simpy Awful Professional Name
Failure at Painting and Sculpture
"Primitive Art" – Shame or Disgrace?
A Dissenting Opinion That Pisses Us Off

5: FAILURE AT WRITING
Sample Bad Opening Lines
Submitting Your Manuscript
Super-Failure in The Novel Form
Failure at Hard-Boiled Dick Pulp Fiction
Failure at Plagiarism
Worst Sellers
Writing and Pitching Screenplays
Vision/Concepts Guaranteed to Get Your Movie Rejected
Catastrophically Failed Screenplays
Unremitting Ethnic Urban Inner-City Streetwise Violence
Unremittingly Sappy Social Commentary Romance
Failure at Poetry
Poem with Rhyme and Form - Sort Of
Literature Failure Through Incomprehensibility

6: FAILING AT EMPLOYMENT AND CAREERS
What's So Great About Working, Anyway?
Nuts and Bolts of Job Failure
You Are Not Necessarily Beaten !
Loser Techniques That Will Set You Free
The Outrageous Resumé Route
Failing Interviewers' Screening Questions
Examples of Losing Interviewee Answers
It's Never Too Late to Fail !
Sample "Thank You" Note

Failing at Keeping a Job You Accidentally Got
Sample Implied Criminality Comments

7 FAILURE IN ADVERTISING AND MARKETING
Built-in Failure Opportunities in a Major Industry
A Look at Specific Departmental Failure Opportunities
Encouragement for Advertising Failure Aspirants

8: FAILURE AT HEALTH AND FITNESS
Health: An Overrated, Outdated Concept
Fitness: Another Hoax Exposed

9: FAILURE AT SCIENCE AND TECHNOLOGY
Science and Technology: Religions of Modern Man
Propositions That Shook the Scientific World – with Laughter !
Biological Conundrums

10: FAILURE AT SPORTS AND MARTIAL ARTS
Sports Need Not Be Fun
Example of a Faux-Sports "Sport"
Getting Real with the Martial Arts

11: FAILURE AT ENTERTAINING and POLITICAL CORRECTNESS
Failure as a Fancy Dinner Host/Hostess
Sample Preciously Presumptuous Menu
Extra Special Case History Section: Food and Beverage Inspectors

12: FAILURE AT ADMINISTRATIVE and LEGAL MATTERS
Comments to Infuriate Selected Officials
Immigration and Customers Inspectors
Extra Special Case History Section:
Food and Beverage Inspectors

13: FAILURE AT BEAUTY and FASHION

EPILOGUE
The Ultimate Step: Failing at Failure Itself

A Final Word

ABOUT THE AUTHOR

WHAT THE READERS SAY

THE COMMERCIAL: MORE BOOKS

DEDICATION

The author wished to dedicate this volume to the Love of his Life -- that glorious lady who endlessly inspires his work and his life; the perfect helpmate in good times and bad.

Unfortunately, he failed to think of anyone who fits that description.

Maybe next book.

AUTHOR'S DISCLAIMER

NOTE: This book was written by professional Losers on a closed course. Readers should not attempt any concept or technique expressed herein without first consulting a qualified Failure expert.

Your Plummeting may vary.

Dean Christopher

The CRITICS SPEAK about Dean Christopher

Fred M. Jafferoni, Military Affairs Editor, *Catholic Badminton Monthly:*
"Every bit as disappointing as I had hoped it would be."

Mary R. Poppings, *Umbrella News:*
"I read it from cover to cover. Some day I plan to read all those pages in between."

Name withheld due to family ties to author:
"He was always such an obstinate child. And now this."

Name withheld due to major film studio affiliation:
"I failed to get the movie rights to this blockbuster."

Mario 'Pavo' Darotti, Artistic Director, *Catskill Opera Company*, South Cairo, NY:
"Sure, sure, but what does he do for an encore?"

PREFACE

HERE'S WHY YOU NEED TO READ THIS BOOK !

We designed *The Loser's Guide To Personal Failure* to be a realist's primer for achieving happiness in these terrible times. It was written to empower readers to cope with, then joyously embrace, their inevitable *Failure* – the personal disaster into which circumstances will unrelentingly force them. This useful *Guide* rebuts vapid pie-in-the-sky panaceas offered by sappy, ineffectual volumes like *Instant Lifelong Investment Success; Land That Babe By Happy Hour* and *Mandelbrot Equations For Dullards*, presenting instead real world strategies to lend meaning to our onrushing doom.

Only an emphatic, unquestionable doom can be satisfying! *Mediocre, everyday, run-of-the-mill failures have nothing to recommend them.* Losing 1-0 at soccer; being shaved 98-97 at basketball; losing a bloodless split decision in the ring; for that matter, having a cuckolded husband murmur to you, "Oh, shucks. Now you just quit that stuff with my wife!" – instead of blasting your house to smoking shreds with rocket propelled grenades – are such mild losses that you might as well never have existed.

Our mission is to teach the *Failure Aspirant* to go down in flames, to *Plummet* to meaningful defeat – to learn to lose joyously, like a grownup!

Today's society, increasingly flooded with mediocre losses of every kind, in every category of defeat, offers little hope for redemption through significant *Personal Failure.* But *The Loser's Guide* does! This scrappy volume, created in the face of raging opposition from the so-called "self help" industry, is like a crackling beacon! It is an explosive source of enlightenment on *Power Failure, Super Failure* and *Comprehensive Catastrophic Failure* – revealed in these pages as the three most practical and realistic hopes for true human happiness.

Students of *The Loser's Guide to Personal Failure* learn that *Failure,* not "success" – as it is usually defined – *is the natural order of things.*

All unhappiness stems from the pointless struggle to achieve "success" – even though "success" is clearly rare, and rarely clear, in *Nature.* Readers learn instead to achieve *Super Failure* – an unexpected form of triumph. They learn not to struggle, but rather to "go with the flow" – indeed how even to go *beyond the* flow of *Failure !*

Individual chapters, written or edited by prominent *Losers,* examine particular *Failure* areas (*Business & Finance, Love & Sex, Health & Fitness, etc.*), so the reader learns from experts' firsthand experience what it takes to become a *Power Loser* in any or all categories! Crisply written, easy-to-understand rules, with practical examples and case histories, etch the principles of *Loser-Think* indelibly onto the synapses of *Failure Aspirants*, who are thereby prepared to ecstatically embrace whatever pathetic fate awaits them.

Our philosophy is elegant in its simplicity:

Failure Is Forever **!**

It can never be taken from you as "success" can.

INTRODUCING FAILURE: SUCCESS IN A MINOR KEY

Basic Failure In Focus

Does the following sound familiar? It ought to, because it's about you!

You are failing miserably. The world is crushing you into helpless little piles of bone powder and meat scum. Your business is in the dumper. Your love life is a tragic punch line. Your hopes and dreams for career advancement; for spiritual fulfillment; for personal health and vigor – all hang by a thread of mucus.

You're in trouble all around. It's amazing you could scrape together enough money to buy this book. If you stole it, it's a miracle you weren't caught. We're amazed that you are even able to read it!

No, your life and your failure *didn't* happen to the other guy – *you* are the loser! Face it. Denial will get you nowhere; it will only cause eventual frustration and rage, maybe even hemorrhoids or an overpowering urge to join the *Republican National Committee.* Accept your defeat consciously, actively, graciously, willingly, aloud. You haven't got a prayer of winning – at least not as the word is usually defined.

We do not say this to make you gloomier than you already are; merely to clarify your situation. Our purpose here is to shock you awake and prepare you for rebirth as a *Power Loser.*

It's better to face life as it really is, no matter how awful. And make no mistake. Life *is* awful. Especially *your* life. It's just not awful *enough* – yet. (Otherwise, why did you read this far? See? You're already getting better – you're admitting there's a problem!)

You may have come close to accepting The Awful Truth during moments when you scream "Life sucks" or "Why me?" (Think about it: why the hell *not* you?) Or in the quiet darkness just before sleep burns its test pattern into the back of your eyelids; when that Voice deep inside, the Voice not entirely your own, reminds you that *Death, Taxes* and *The Home Shopping Network* will eventually claim us all.

But if you are really disturbed by your inevitable *Failure*, then you are still suffering from "old think." We'll change all that. *The Loser's Guide To Personal Failure* will teach you how to make the most of your descent into despair. Soon we will convert all your anxiety into esctasy.

Soon you will learn the secret of *Plummeting* to happiness!

A Brief History Of Failure

Throughout the millennia, the *Power Elite* has kept the masses in the dark about the secret benefits of Failure. For their own sinister purposes they have pretended that something called "success" is possible – even desirable – for ordinary people. Can you just imagine how naive they think we are? They have persistently fabricated "success stories" and other hype so they can (a) Sell "success" books and seminars, and (b) Divert our attention from the real-world importance of *Losing*.

Even in America we have been regularly duped by government, by advertising, by false prophets. It's a conspiracy of the "success" lobby, whose books, tapes and seminars preach that the way to happiness is the thing called "success". They teach us steps to this "success." But the clear-eyed among us see that this is a sneaky diversionary tactic designed to keep us off the sweet scent of *Failure*!

But think of it. You're a nobody. *They* are somebodies. They already have most of the cookies. Why in the world would *they* share them? Why would they tell *you or me* where *Life's True Gold* is hidden? They are as shifty as the dickens. They want you to believe that *their* steps to "success" are better than *your* steps. But they lie. Besides, it is not only the steps, but also the *goal* they promote, that is *wrong!* That explains why nobody is really happy – even those who enjoy so-called "success." We believe that nearly all "success"-oriented material is deliberately misleading. Popular bestsellers such as

- *Dare to Be Wider*
- *Selfishness = Smallmouth Bass 4U!*
- *Auto-Stimulate Your Way to Mega-Sexuality*
- *Deeply Thin Zen Tennis Success*
- *Happiness via Power Eructation*
- *Seven Days To Super Tallness!*
- *Winning Through Savagery*
- *Vomit Your Way To Super Health!*

- *Commando Toughness ... No Training!*
- *Date Glamour Queens By 7:00 P.M.!*
- *Hole-In-One Golf: Score 18 Every Time!*

... *et cetera*, are pure baloney. That's because they are based on the flawed premise that *Natural Losers* – including you and me – can become *Non-Losers*.

Poppycock! Tommyrot! Pshaw! That's like saying that a muskrat can become an astronaut or an Oldsmobile. It's just not in our genes. What *is* possible is to take *Potential Losers* – even you – and convert them into *Power-Losers*, and in some cases, into *Super-Losers*. That's what *The Loser's Guide to Personal Failure* can accomplish for you, starting this very minute! Ready to transform yourself? Ready to awaken your Inner Loser? Are you ready to learn *Power-Failure?*

Then read on – and learn to *Plummet !*

The Truth Will Help You Fail

If you've read this far, you obviously have what it takes to face the *Real Truth.* And here it is. It's important, so pay attention. Underline things if necessary; it's your book.

The Real Truth: Just as entropy (breakdown, dissipation, decay, death, grinding to a halt) is the central principle of the universe, by extension *failure is the natural state of mankind !* It's baked right into our species. It is the very stuff of which DNA is made. There is nothing we can do about it.

Chaos, not order, is what universal life truly aspires to, and what it always accomplishes in the end.

Translation: flunking out is what humans are programmed for, because we are part of nature.

Can You Handle This Bold Implication ?

The proper metaphor for *real life* is *not* (as often claimed in "self-help" books) football, baseball, golf or other carefully regulated sports. It is *bungee jumping* – the primitive ritual that follows the *real life* rules of physics, terror and sudden impending doom. Here is an activity that requires no phony "skills" – just the *real life* experience, in real time, of gravity and your own stampeding adrenalin. Bungee jumping requires no sissified conceits like fielding grounders, tackling beefy opponents or putting for a birdie.

It is as simple and as direct as mud: you tie a thong to your leg and leap headfirst from some horrifyingly high place. Bungee jumping (Falling = Flailing = "Failing" – get it?) downward at high speed – is *Nature* in action! *Plummeting* is instructive; it is unforgiving and immediate. It is ... *real.* The only more perfect metaphor for real life would be jumping *without* the bungee – *Total Plummet !*

Few attain this level of *Failure* and live to talk about their happiness. But some inspired people learn to jump with the thong around their necks, so to speak. These *Truly Aware* people follow Nature's way and *Plummet.* These are the genuine *Super-Failers !*

Alas, not everyone is born with the inspired deficiencies that let them *Plummet* straight to the bottom. Few indeed are *Natural Plummeters.* Even *you* may not qualify for that distinction. But here's the good news: by making the most of what you haven't; through hard work and by reading this book (or having someone read it to you) every day; you, too, can achieve more *Failure* than most *naturally* deficient people!

We can – and will – *accelerate* and *intensify* any loser's "loserness," until he or she has reached his/her/its

Maximum Failure Potential (MFP). At that point all frustration and rage evaporate. True happiness seeps into the *Loser's* awareness. It is *real life nirvana* – extinction of all desire for, or pretense of, "success." It is release. It is pure *Plummet.*

Realization of MFP is the joyous achievement of *Power Failure*: the ecstasy that waits at the end of the bungee tether!

Step With Us Now Onto The Highway To Failure !

Before we begin our descent, some basic definitions:

- *Plummeting:* The process of dropping straight down, usually very quickly. This can happen mentally, spiritually, morally, financially, politically, physically, in golf ... or *any or all of the above.* We especially encourage *Comprehensive Plummeting.*

- *Power-Failure:* Plummeting rapidly to the depths and losing all hope for any chance of "success" in a chosen category of personal activity, with *little expectation of reversal.*

- *Super-Failure:* Plummeting extremely rapidly and publicly to the *extreme* depths and losing all hope for, or chance of, "success" in a chosen category of personal activity, with *no possibility of reversal.*

- *Comprehensive Catastrophic Failure (CCF):* Plummeting *astonishingly rapidly and publicly* to the depths, even *below* the depths, and losing all hope for, chance of, or even desire for, "success" in *any and all* categories of personal activity, with *no* possibility of reversal – indeed, with every likelihood of *extreme, cataclysmic, chronic, smelly and progressive worsening of one's personal situation forever.*

Yes indeed. Doom, Hell, Horror, Total Loss! *CCF* also affects everyone around you. Friends, family, passers-by, everyone whose life you touch: all turn into stupid, piggish, incompetent candidates for self-inflicted exit wounds made by hollow-point ammo. *CCF* is attained by barely 4% of all *Loser's Guide* graduates – but it *is* possible!

Do *You* Have What It Takes To Plummet?

Please never forget that *Plummeting* is the key to our method, the essential secret of our technique. It is constantly to be aspired to. It is the secret of happiness. To reach your *Maximum Personal Failure (MPF)* as quickly and emphatically as possible is what *Plummeting* is all about.

Since *all* progress toward *Failure* depends upon mastery of *Plummeting*, any activity or thinking that does not contribute substantially to development of this skill is of no use to our quest, and should be carefully avoided. It is wise, in this connection, to stop memorizing sports statistics; knowing the names of "lead guitarists" in look-alike, sound-alike popular music groups; or chairmen of Senate sub-committees; or which countries belong to NATO.

Here's How To Use This Book

- *Read and believe absolutely everything written here*. It's your only realistic hope for achieving the kinds of *Failure* that bring true happiness. Remember that other books are bursting with mistakes, half-truths and outright lies. Some will print cheerful attractive pictures and catchy slogans to lure you off the *Failure Path.* The "success" conspiracy never sleeps. *They* are out there, and unless you're careful they will get you. In fact, unless you read this book, it's almost certain.

- *Master the ideas you learn here by putting them into immediate and constant practice*. It's only when *Failure* becomes part of your automatic behavior that you'll be able to fail *at will !*

- *Never forget your ultimate Goal: Comprehensive Catastrophic Failure (CCF)*. Always remember the doorway to that Goal:

Learn, Learn, Learn
and
Practice, Practice, Practice!

- *Memorize our illustrative proverbs and anecdotes and repeat them* aloud whenever you arc with anyone, whether or not they are *Failure Aspirants*. You never can tell where your next brother or sister *Power Loser* will come from!

- *Ineptitude is important.* Avoid any situation that's apt to make you ept. Ineptitude (sometimes called "ineptness") in every endeavor is appropriate at all times—with *one exception.* Although it is wise to cultivate *Sloth, Inattention* and *Slovenly Behavior* of every kind, *efficiency IS permitted* while learning the lessons of this volume, and practicing them diligently!

- *Start modestly.* Don't ask too much of yourself. Start with baby steps, embryonic steps ... true *Failure* prodigies have been known to begin with *zygote steps !* It is never too early to master the elements of *Failure.*

- Learn to fail in one category at a time. *Do not try for Comprehensive Catastrophic Failure* right off the bat. Time and patience are required for major self-destruction. But *CCF* is guaranteed if you follow the rules of this book, and remember to Practice, Practice, Practice!

- *... and Tell, Tell, Tell all your friends* about *The Loser's Guide to Personal Failure. Do not fail* (we're being ironic – ha ha ha!) to check your local paper frequently for the date, time and place of our live in-person *Loser's Guide Seminars*, coming soon to your town, computer screen or expensive and complicated handheld device! (Sorry, we can no longer offer free refreshments at our events.)

CHAPTER ONE

GENERIC FAILURE

by

The Authors

Ready? Let's begin by examining the basic notion of *Failure* – what it is and how to accomplish it. All the lessons here reveal the principles of specific *Failures* studied later, so be sure to learn them well.

There are many areas in which to fail.

Failure is an equal opportunity process!

As suggested earlier, the *Failure Aspirant* can choose to seal his/her fate in many categories, including (but not limited to) *Business, Marriage, Sports, Health, Golf, Politics, Filial Duty* – why, *Failure* is limited only by one's imagination and one's *will to fail!*

Failure Is A Many-Faceted Jewel

Anything you can "succeed" at can as easily become "a gem of a failure" once you know how! There are as many failures as there are individuals who fail. Surely there are even failings and *Failures* as yet undreamed-of, beckoning from beyond the horizon.

Yet all failures share certain basic attributes. In dissecting *The Anatomy Of Failure,* we quickly see that all *Failures* contain some combination of these nine (9) elements:

1. Not enough something
2. Too much something
3. Something too soon
4. Something too late
5. Wrong thing said
6. Wrong thing done
7. Wrong decision taken
8. You look funny

9. You make other people (or powerful, aggressive animals)

- Angry
- Jealous
- Sad
- Frustrated
- Hurt
- Scared
- Disgusted, or
- Late for something they want to be early to.

All these components can be intermingled to create some situation that, properly managed, will produce your desired *Failure*. For example, let's say that you want to fail at *Making a Good Martini Cocktail.* The failure to make a "good" martini has its roots in the categories:

- *Wrong Thing Done* (i.e., the bad martini itself, and/or the decision to make a martini in the first place) and
- *Too Much Something* (probably vermouth).

Of course this also implies the factors:

- *Wrong Decision Taken* (e.g., the decision to add vermouth) and
- *Make Others ... Disgusted* (when they sip the bad martini).

By extension this might be said also to include:

- *Not Enough Something* (i.e., not enough restraint with the vermouth).

The student can see how closely interrelated *Failure Factors* can be! It is therefore important to learn to recognize the interplay of these factors, the better to orchestrate their potentialities into the discordant symphony that will be your own personal *Failure!*

To engineer a specific failure, the *Failure Aspirant* need simply tailor *Generic Failure Factors* to the specifications of the *Failure Category* desired. The above example is a good example of *Double Failure*:

- *Failure at Bartending* – and by extension
- *Failure as a Dinner Party Host/Hostess.*

CASE HISTORY:
Interplay Of Failure Factors In Action

Let's study a specific example. "Morty" (not his real name) and "Ferruccio" (not his real name either) were candidates for an open membership at the Piffwell Hills Country Club (not its real name). One would "succeed" in passing the Membership Committee, and one would Fail. In reviewing this case history, note how skillfully the Loser "mixed and matched" the *Generic Failure Factors* to accomplish this *Power-Failure.* Can you guess which one Failed?

"Morty" showed up precisely on time. He wore conservative grey slacks, a blue blazer, white tailored shirt and muted necktie. He was clean shaven, exuding a whiff of *Polo™.* Morty waited until the Committee Secretary invited him into the Board Room, then entered smiling, shook hands all around, but waited to be invited before sitting. He sat politely and answered all their questions with cheer and with quiet aplomb. He admitted to long term success in business; many community activitics; fondness for golf. He did not smoke. After the interview, he thanked everyone for their consideration of his application and left quietly to await their decision.

"Ferruccio" arrived 48 minutes late, parked his dented smoking 1979 Oldsmobile *Toronado* on the lawn, visible through the Board Room windows. He wore a frayed maroon terrycloth robe stained with old egg salad, recent egg salad, *Gallo White Zinfandel* and an unidentified thick brownish splotch on the right sleeve. He had not shaved or bathed for days, maybe weeks, and carried a severed lamb's head under one arm. His robe pocket overflowed with used *Kitty Litter.*

Ferruccio barged through the closed Board Room doors and angrily insisted upon immediate attention, although the Committee was in the midst of their coffee-and-finger-sandwich break. "Whaddya think, I've got all day, you snot-weasels?" he screamed, yanking "Buzz" (his real name) Terwilliger's lapel. Sprawling into "Biff" (his real nickname) Blodgett's chair, "Ferruccio" proceeded to pull gobs of yellowish-green mucus out of his nostrils, roll them into tiny lopsided balls and flick them across the room.

He smoked a 75-cent cigar, chewed tobacco and spat glistening tawny lungers onto the carpet and paintings of English hunting scenes. He loudly related how badly he had been "screwed over by every goddam boss" he had ever had; how that "intolerant bitch he was married to" left him just because of "one lousy incident with a Brownie Troop"; how he thought golf was boring as hell but it might at least give him a chance to scrounge some bucks off rich WASPs and meet some new babes to "plow."

Standing up abruptly, he shouted "Holy crap, it's nearly noon; I gotta get my clothes outa there afore Big Mama Gladine's husbands get back!" Bolting from the room he asked for his locker key right away, to save time when he came back for Happy Hour.

If you guessed that "Ferruccio" was the one *Plummeting* toward *Power-Failure,* you guessed right! Bravo(a)!

Examine the *Failure Factors* he so skillfully combined to guarantee the Committee's decision, and list them in your workbook.

CHAPTER TWO

FAILURE AT LOVE AND SEX
by Werner Oberfaulk, M.D., Ph.D., C.P.A.

Dr. Oberfaulk is the Heinrich Gorfft Professor of Vertebrate Sexuality at Hochloch University in Dreddloch, Germany. Internationally acclaimed for his controversial 1998 best seller Ten Days to Random Erections, *he writes and lectures throughout Europe and North America on a wide range of psychosexual topics, often in comprehensible languages. He is tall and stooped, with a greying beard, and frequently interrupts his presentations with short, sharp bursts of laughter, never explained.*

Dr. Oberfaulk claims to have loved and lost more women than any living German. This chapter, written originally in English, was translated into German by one of his associates, from German into Spanish by another, then finally back into English by a third. The only known example of such a "triple blind translation," Dr. Oberfaulk said the procedure was done for good reason, which he did not reveal. Suddenly he laughed sharply and left the room. All laughter has been expunged from the text for purposes of continuity. – The Editors

Of all human emotional relationships, the most important one is the *Love Relationship.* It involves close – sometimes even permanent – association with a "Significant Other," "Lover," "Life Partner," occasionally even a "Spouse." Its early stages feature an activity called "Sex," sometimes (but not necessarily) associated with the *Love Relationship.*

Sex has been widely publicized. A great many people know something about it, so it requires no further description here. Suffice to define it as a clumsy, often tiring, yet relatively pleasurable substitute for sneezing. In males it relieves pelvic congestion; in females it breaks up the day and leads to acquisition of many credit cards. Both genders ultimately prefer it in moderation – men before watching sports or sleeping; women after shopping for costly clothing.

Sex is uncomfortable, but possible, while marching, doing your daily calisthenics or invading nearby countries with fertile fields and well-rounded peasant girls. But we digress. *Love/Sex* is useful because (a) Species continuation (although a debatable benefit) depends upon sexual connection; and (b) We are conditioned to base our self-esteem upon acceptance by (and physical prowess with) the opposite sex.

Of course some people base their self-esteem on dealings with the same sex; or with both sexes or any combination of sexes. That in no way alters the *Rules of Failure.* Because of this linkage with *Self-Image*, the possibility of failure at *Love/Sex* is a serious concern for most people. Everyone wants to "succeed" at any cost. We, personally, fail to understand this concept.

Love – Fraud Or Delusion?

Throughout history, often in psychiatric studies, we see evidence of people's (even German people's!) urgent need to be "loved." The drive to "succeed" at Love – or at least at Sex – plays a dominant role in Mythology, Classical Literature, Renaissance Painting, Sculpture and Daytime TV Serials. Men and women regularly abandon truly substantive matters in order to pursue *Love/Sex Objects.* Many go to great lengths to snare their prey. They compose symphonies or sonnets; travel extreme distances in Coach Class; endure unimaginable hardships and/or monetary loss; sob late at night with shoulders heaving up and down, up and down; and in general make complete asses of themselves – all to "succeed" at Love. They are such repulsive little slugs.

For what does their "success" ultimately deliver? A night of questionably enjoyable writhing and grinding. Pouagh! Pouagh! Weekends at the beach. A fraternity pin, later a gleaming engagement ring, probably purchased at a Discount Outlet. An ultimately inconclusive ski vacation to an overpriced resort swarming with bland people – insurance adjustors; saucy-buttocked pharmaceutical representatives with rolling sample cases; a biblical scholar from a local community college and his pasty, unappetizing wife. We repeat, Pouagh!

Then the inevitable pathetic bourgeois marriage, attended by relatives one barely remembers or likes. Wedding gifts one barely recognizes or likes. I mean – *two* fondue sets? An asparagus steamer? A *chafing dish*?

It gets worse. Soon, the predictable cottage in the suburbs, complete with bad plumbing, crabgrass and a mortgage. Shortly thereafter, screaming infants and toddlers with nappies bulging with greenish smelly poo poo. In-laws who drain the "successful couple" of their substance, all the while complaining about their faults. Finally: uncomfortable bedtimes, headaches, shout-outs, tense meetings with overpriced divorce lawyers.

Emotional and financial ruin. Then, one day ... a new *Love/Sex Object* appears. These silly worms make me spew. Will they *never* learn?

"Success" in *Love/Sex* is demonstrably either *Temporary Vanity* or *Permanent Hoax.* The obvious route to happiness is to avoid it altogether or, absent that, to move on to the relief of *Sexual Super Failure* as quickly as possible. Following is an effective strategy for failing at *Love/Sex,* so you can quickly move ahead to gratifying *Self-Pity,* and the delicious secondary benefit of knowing that your "romance" was doomed all along.

Strategic Approaches To Failure At Love/Sex

The most reliable road around romance is *via Power Repulsiveness.*

[Note: All Repulsiveness *is an effective tool, and can lead to, e.g.,* Failure To Get VP Status *at ad agencies or in other WASP-dominated institutions (such as* Mary Kay Cosmetics *or the Detroit auto industry). Clearly* Power Repulsiveness *is best used in moderation. One wishes to stay alive, after all. – The Editors]*

Failure Through Power Repulsiveness

This topic is of wide application, easily transferable to many potential *Failure* categories. Read on.

Although virtually all humans are repulsive to one degree or another, in one way or another, to master *Power Repulsiveness* requires assiduous cultivation. It is not an easy state to achieve in a society conditioned to the ephemeral and un-natural trappings of personal "pleasantness" and "attractiveness," which is to say, a world influenced by California culture and teenage fashion magazines.

Luckily, most of us already have *at least some repulsive attributes* worth developing: physical, behavioral or mental qualities that can be developed to *Power Repel* others – once we learn how. We are not all created equal in *Repulsiveness*, but we can all learn to make the most of whatever potential vile, unappetizing or obnoxious qualities we may possess.

When it comes to repelling potential lovers, the basic assets at our disposal fall into three areas:

- Physical
- Financial
- Behavioral

Usually *Repulsiveness* in any two of these areas is sufficient to guarantee losing a relationship with a *Love/Sex Object.* In rare cases, just one well-placed *Mega-Repulsion* can do it. But the beginner is urged to work patiently for across-the-board, steady progress in all three categories. Far better to achieve *Balanced Repulsiveness* and be *sure* to lose, than to gamble on a quick *Plummet* in only one *Repulsiveness* category.

Body Weight and Physical Repulsion

Specifics vary, but in general, glaring abnormalities in body weight - morbidly obese or famine-bony - reliably speed up the *Failure Process,* since both extremes are generally considered unappealing. Men generally consider mega-skeletal or hyper-upholstered women sexually unacceptable. So a *Power Failure* in either state will produce an instant one-category victory for women seeking to repel men. All they need do is *Power-Starve* or *Power-Eat* (preferably while avoiding exercise).

Men find it much harder to *Power Fail* in the weight category. This is because so many women have trouble disqualifying any man – be he sparrow-chested with arms like *Dill's Pipe Cleaners* or a blimp-faced, hassock-bellied lardbucket – unless he also revolts her *via Power-Failure* in the *Financial* category.

Height, Length and Physical Repulsion

Not much can be done about inherent qualities such as physical dimension, although male *Failure Aspirants* desperate to be short enough to repulse women sometimes have their legs and/or spines surgically shortened. In drastic instances, fellows eager for *Instant Failure* also undergo penis reduction operations, sizing down to inconsiderability virtually within seconds.

General Appearance and Physical Repulsion

For over 75 years cosmetic surgeons, responding to the public's mistaken desire for "success through beauty," have reduced and shaped noses, increased breast size (especially in women) and tightened their patients' wrinkled faces into grotesque masks resembling drum-tight parchment. (Cf. Joan Rivers; Mickey Rourke; numberless Park Avenue matrons who lend their frequently hyphenated names to the boards of muesums and landmine removal foundations.) Today surgeons are free to turn their attention to the natural work of skin loosening, bosom flattening and building bulky macaw-like noses for *Failure*-bound patients of all sexes.

Hygiene, "Low-Giene" and Physical Repulsion

"Cleanliness is next to godliness," is what we are told as kids, and it's what most of us are hoodwinked into believing as adults. Happily, this otherwise meaningless proverb at least implies a sure-fire technique for ungodly *Failure* in *Love/Sex*:

Be Dirty !

Remember, *Nature* provides continual – perhaps even endless – opportunities for bodily filth, but virtually *no natural cleansing* other than exposing oneself to intense rain whipped by exceptionally high winds!

What does *that* tell you about *Nature's Plan*?

Humans inherently exude vileness and stench from every body opening. Without the *un-natural* processes of showering, brushing teeth and wiping our nether bits, we would remain naturally dirty all over. From this it follows that the more "natural" we are, the better our chances of offending a potential *Love/Sex Object.* Try it yourself. Go for just one week without wiping, brushing, shaving (yes, ladies too!) or bathing ... and watch others back quickly away. Really – it works!

For especially difficult cases, you may find it necessary to go outside for supplementary "low-gienic" unpleasantness. For instance, in case your *Love/Sex*

Object has a damaged olfactory nerve, and isn't affected by your stink, you will have to rely upon the *visual aspects of filth.*

Putting Theory Into Practice

Here's a tip. Smear your face and hands with the dung of domestic animals (which is more widely available than that of wild animals, and much safer to acquire). Crumple leaves and twig bits into your matted hair. Roll around in fresh macadam or soft mud until your skin and clothes are caked with gunk. *Your Love/Sex Object*'s eyes will surely get the idea! (Note that the effect is best when these materials are still wet and therefore more easily transferable to the skin and clothing of the *Love/Sex Object.* But like pond scum, even when dry they make their point, which is that you are putrefaction itself – and well on your way to *Power-Failure* in the important *Love/Sex* category!)

Wardrobe, Grooming and Physical Repulsiveness

"Clothes make the man," bleats a timeless dictum. "Dress for success," scream traditional establishment "self-help" books – as if "success" were something to be desired! But once again, this dull conventional advice, though based upon a faulty premise, contains an inverse wisdom that, properly put to use, can help us *fail*; to wit:

Dress Badly !

Ideally one would not dress at all, but public nudity is difficult to get away with. In private with the *Love/Sex Object*, especially during those first few meetings, stripping off all clothes and displaying one's (preferably filthy – see above) naked (preferably grossly overweight or pathetically skeletal – see even further above) body is usually a giant step towards *Love/Sex Failure.*

But even in public situations when clothing is *de rigueur*, you need not be defeated: you can always rely on clothes that are:

- Terminally dirty and tattered
- Irretrievably tasteless, outmoded or inappropriate; and/or
- Any combination of the above (in extreme cases).

Let's take a closer look at this solution.

Dirty, Tattered Clothes And Repulsion

This is an extension of "low-giene," as applied to garments. It speaks volumes about your *Social Acceptabilty. Luckily, there are many ways to foul garments.* Human excretions (urine, nasal mucus, fecal matter, vomitus) will cling stubbornly to most garments, especially old cloth with worn and broken fibers. Obviously the same goes for animal detritus, fresh blood, marsh muck and so much more. Go ahead. Use your imagination! There are many effective ways to apply filth – often simply loading pockets with rodent puke or maggoty road kill will do the trick!

Bold New Dimensions In Tastelessness

Even when clean, certain garments send up a "red flag" to the *Love/Sex Object,* based solely on the garments *per se.* To appear in public in beltless expandable brown *Dacron*™ pants and white leatherino loafers (even without the matching belt) is enough to drive many potential partners shrieking from your zip code. When even more "punch" is required, bold men might experiment by wearing their mothers' Donna Reed (or elder sisters' Condoleezza Rice) dresses; Grandad's double-breasted overcoat with knee stockings; or perhaps a Nehru jacket, tie-dye bell-bottoms and love beads. (A tangle of gold chains around the neck ought to deliver instant failure, especially if they are tangled in an off-center *Chest Merkin*, but results are mixed, particularly in California's Porsche communities.)

Women are advised to try baseball umpires' chest protectors; Bermuda shorts or flower print toreador pants – anything that makes them look like a featured guest on an afternoon TV "reality" *Shocking Confessions* show.

The simple fact of:

- Wearing any of the above; and
- Wearing it in public

... virtually guarantees the wearer quick *Power-Failure !*

In difficult cases, where the *Love/Sex Object* is immunized by dint of extreme inborn tastelessness, a much higher degree of wardrobe action will be called for. This requires *Special Effects Costuming*, some of which can be created by the *Failure Aspirant,* but most of which must come from professionals. Examples of effective outfits include, but are not limited to:

- *Crotchless ski pants*
- *Balsa wood nun's habit*
- *Banlon™ shirts with attached foxtails*
- *Chain mail codpiece*

- *Mackerel skin underpants (3-ply)*
- *"Living Suspenders" (Flat eels or mature tapeworms)*
- *Half a horse costume (Choose your half!)*
- *4-Foot Fingernails*
- *Gay alien outfit (Extraterrestrial)*
- *Gay alien outfit (Undocumented Earthling)*
- *... and so much more*

Be bold. Be daring. Be tasteless. Be outrageous – you have nothing to lose but your enslavement of the illusion of "success"!

Failing At Financial Solvency = Failing At Love/Sex

Good news: empty coffers are your friends!

Evidence of financial deficiency is an excellent element to leverage for *Power Failure* in the *Love/Sex* category. If you are lucky enough to be truly penniless and in debt, you need only *loudly and frequently remind a potential partner of your fiscal situation.* Blatantly avoid any situation where you might have to spend money on the *Love/Sex Object.* After a very short time, usually a matter of hours, he/she will get the idea and *Failure* will come bounding your way. (Frequent requests for small loans can help get the point across even sooner!)

For those burdened by wealth, or even solvency, there are two strategies:

- *Pretend to be poor,* and do your best to act like the impecunious people you have seen or read about. *Warning: this approach can be exhausting.* It requires the constant effort of keeping your *Love/Sex Object* isolated from your real life and all its houses, cars, twin-engine Cessnas, stacked copies of The *Robb Report* on your Heppelwhite coffee table, wealthy friends, etc. You will need to maintain a separate "poor" wardrobe, and possibly (distasteful as it may seem at first) cultivate really poor "friends." You may have to shun Republican bridge partners and stay away from the Country Club for days at a time. There is also the bother of renting a secondary run-down residence stocked with rats, roaches and old vinyl LPs of music by the underclass – possibly even buying audiocassettes or, to go all the way, 8-track tapes. Still, if you relish a challenge, this is the way to go!

- *Spend, lose or give away all your money.* "Method Poverty" is quite effective. With a little effort you can find *non-Failure-Oriented* people willing to take away some or all of your wealth. The more publicly and noisily they acquire your money, the better – since that will help you appear a complete fool in the eyes of your *Love/Sex Object.* This has the advantage of propelling you instantly into *Loser-Think*, because you will have experienced *real life loss.* Your resultant *Self-Hate* will give you energy to apply against *other* categories in which you seek *Failure!*

Time Off For Bad Behavior

"Behave yourself," hissed Mom many years ago, and in the end we all heed her exhortation. Good behavior gets you goodies. Bad behavior gets you slapped. It gets you detention. It gets you ostracized. It gets you ... *Failure !*

Just what you want. "Born and raised in the briar patch!"

Learn to *behave badly* and you will more easily march on toward *Power Failure.* Bad behavior (especially from fiscally diminished, filthy, physically repulsive people wearing stupid clothes) is a major factor in achieving *Power Failure.* When mastered, it can even *Plummet* the aspirant down the chute into the ranks of the *Super-Failers.* This is nowhere more true than in the category of

Love/Sex. For the sake of convenience we divide this study into two categories:

- Etiquette (Bad things to do); and
- Speech (Bad things to say)

The student who masters the combined use of these tools will quickly accomplish his goal in virtually *any Failure* category.

Anti-Etiquette Is The New Etiquette

Etiquette for years was the exclusive province of *Success Aspirants*, and their deluded hangers-on. Its rules dealt with politeness (not always appropriate) and social acceptability (unnecessary in the world of *Losers*). But for our purposes it is necessary to expand etiquette to encompass *Failure Modality*. We pass along these *Helpful Hints* to aid in the swift destruction of any budding *Love/Sex Relationship.* (Due to space limitations we can touch only upon main points.)

Failure At The Dinner Table

Forget everything you ever learned about manners. That was the *Old Etiquette* – so *Yesterday!* There is only one rule: enjoy the food, and let your *Love/Sex Object* see your enjoyment. If digestive noises (oral or otherwise) and grunting, moaning, singing or other sound effects add to your enjoyment, so much the better. Remember that *yours* is the only pleasure that matters! So make lots of noise. It is a compliment to the chef.

Disregard disapproving glances from the unenlightened. They will never be as happy in "success" as you will be in *Failure.* It is natural to go face down into the food, particularly liquid or sloshy foods. If it does not burn the front of your face, let your head *Plummet* into the food. It's an apt metaphor for your life. Anything distasteful should be spat onto the table, into your host's lap on onto nearby pets.

Respect your own pleasure! Do not hesitate to play with your meal if it feels good, or if it will draw additional negative attention to you. Throwing it, juggling with it or slipping it into the garments and accessories of your *Love/Sex Object* and other dinner companions can also be immensely satisfying.

Should you feel the need to evacuate your bladder or bowels while at table, by no means rein in what is a completely natural (and life-affirming) bodily function – the excretion of poisons. This process offers a philosophical symmetry to dining – noisily ingesting food from one end of the body while noisily expelling *previously* ingested food from the other. This is truly thought-provoking. It makes a statement about time and matter. Of such balances is *Power-Failure* made.

And memorable dining experiences, too.

Failure Through Visiting

A great deal of our social lives is spent calling on others. Indeed, the Etiquette involved in whom one sees, and under what circumstances, is a major plot point in classic Russian and French novels. Although the authors may be unreasonably concerned with the appropriateness of such social contacts, we are not. After all, they are foreigners, probably destined for "success" and happiness. We are under no such constraints.

Indeed, we scorn their obsessive concern with such exaggerated, indeed neurotic, correctness. We say as follows*: visit anyone you damn please, whether you know them or not, whether you are invited or not.* Many people simply do not have the time to invite others, so by all means feel free to relieve them of that cumbersome responsibility. Barge right in. Use or take anything you want – any truly generous host wouldn't have it any other way.

Should you encounter resistance, real or imagined, be aggressive and resist anyone who tries to impede your plunge toward *Failure.* Release your hosts' exquisite rare birds and exotic tropical fish back into the wild. Invite the hostess out behind the garage for a few feverish intimate moments. Disregard the anguished cries of your host or of your *Love/Sex Object.*

It is a true joy – greatly undervalued – to visit people whom you do not know, have never even heard of and will probably never see again. It astonishes them, and provides new things for you to steal (especially upstairs!). Do not overlook medicine chests and antique wardrobes.

Bereavements

When there is a death in the family of someone you know, remind them that people who die *should* die – or else obviously they *wouldn't !* Who's in charge here anyway – the patient or *Nature?* This adds dimension to their thinking and works wonders shuffling the ever-changing deck of your acquaintances.

At the funeral or memorial service, repeat for everyone the many dirty jokes the deceased told in your presence.

This is another way of sharing her/his life with others. If you can remember the names of persons he/she bedded out of wedlock (especially if your *Love/Sex Object* was one of them), this is the perfect time to make a clean breast of it on behalf of the deceased. It will lighten everyone's sadness and convert it into something very different. Drink lots of liquor and mutter "Good riddance to bad rubbish" whenever relatives are nearby. Pocket nearby *Hummels* and other *bric-à-brac* for display at your own impending funeral.

Weddings

Drink lots of liquor and mutter "Good riddance to bad rubbish" (a widely useful expression, as seen above) whenever the bride walks past, especially if you are on the bride's side of the aisle. Be sure to offer your hip flask to her relatives during the repeating of the vows.

When the clergyman asks the traditional question "... whether anyone knows just cause why this man and woman should not be joined in holy matrimony," shout out "Because she's carrying my child, that *slut!*"

What a funny prank! A few people may laugh nervously, but most will gasp in genuine horror. Always drive your own car to these events.

Other Religious Occasions

At church, temple or other religious gathering for the first time with the *Love/Sex Object* and his/her family, repeatedly shrieking out "What hugger-mugger!" and "Did you ever see such blatant *hypocrisy?"* virtually guarantees near-term *Failure.* If the father is extremely wealthy and influential, you might even *Plummet* directly to *Super Failure* in a very short time.

- Useful hint: almost any reprehensible behavior that will ensure notoriety will be viewed as *even more* despicable and revolting in otherwise "pious" circumstances. Ungodly actions are taken very seriously by the godly.

CASE HISTORY:
Sample Opening Lines To Hasten Failure At Love/Sex

- *When you meet her, make your first words "Hey, speaking of Shostakovich ... "*
- *Ladies: meeting a new man at a party, cry out loudly, "You know, size really DOES matter!"*
- *Wear a thick sweater with holes cut to reveal your armpits, and whisper, "Ever seen pit thatches like THAT, baby?"*
- *Attach a toy fox terrier to your fly with a safety pin. Never explain.*
- *Show her an 18"x24" color enlargement of your penis while whistling "Something Wonderful" from The King & I.*
- *Ask him if he prefers "Alligator style" or "The old fashioned 'Inquisition Rack'."*
- *Smile mysteriously and ask if her purse is watertight.*
- *Express disappointment that he doesn't have his bankbook with him.*
- *If asked "What's your sign?" reply either "Slow – School Crossing" or "Feces, With Herpes Rising."*

Feel free to mix and match, and to experiment with the above techniques. Remember that any excess indulged in conscientiously and enthusiastically, in the quest for *Failure* in *Love Sex*, is justified.

Shame is for the weak; and "success" is not an option. Good luck.

CHAPTER THREE

FAILURE IN BUSINESS AND FINANCE

by F. Barry Pifkin

F. Barry Pifkin came up from nothing. By age 11, however, he had put his father through nursing school and built a far-flung financial empire, based on profits from a milk money pyramid scheme he developed while still in elementary school.

But the Securities Exchange Commission *eventually discovered his trick of buying Greek* drachmas, *renaming them "dollars" and convincing the elderly and the blind to buy them as real American dollars. Based upon the* drachma's *astronomical exchange rate, his personal* Return On Investment *was consistently above 87,000%. His coffers swelled to overflowing. The young "Crown Prince of Hyper-Exchange" was on his way to becoming the legendary "King of the Jerk Bonds." He rode an express comet to* Power Failure *during his subsequent meteoric* Plummet *across the international financial firmament during the 1990's and greed-drenched early 2000's.*

The first Fiscal Power Failure *actually to be executed for "egregious monetary outrages" (including computer theft of all the money in Benelux), Pifkin wrote this essay exactly a week before his only trip to the gas chamber in 2002, which was later unaccountably declared a suicide by the* International Monetary Fund.

Based on his speech to the New York Stock Exchange *(which was also the backbone of his defense in the since disbanded* World Court Fiscal Tribunal*), this chapter outlines the principles of* Comprehensive Catastrophic Failure in Business and Finance *more convincingly than any document in the history of commercial literature. That the principles outlined herein led directly to his death is convincing testimony to the thrilling irreversibility of Pifkin's* CCF, *which will live forever in the annals of* Super Failure. – *The Editors.*

"Money talks," as the saying goes. For once, they're right. If there is any one universally accepted indicator of "success," it is monetary wealth. In fact, most people equate money directly with "success." For them, the two concepts are inseparable and co-equal. Money is power; it is both symbol and proof of "success." Logically therefore, the *lack* of money is a prime definition of *Failure.* What better way to trumpet your *Plummeting Failure* than to be able to boast that you have *no money?*

[NOTE: See Chapter Two's section Empty Coffers Are Your Friends *for advice that is as valid for Failing in Business/Finance as it is for Love/Sex! –The Editors]*

Empty pockets – especially for a man – are as time-honored a disincentive to romance as Aerosol Vagina Repellent. Clearly the same goes for all social and business interactions. The instant any potential associate, benefactor or victim knows that you have no money, and no fabulously wealthy, loving relatives clinging threadily to life on a ventilator at their local HMO, your chances of "success" will evaporate faster than a sex addict's chastity pledge at the Adult Video Convention.

But even if you start with the handicap of having a sound financial picture (or the illusion of one), do not be discouraged. You can still find ways to *Plummet* in *Business and Finance.*

Let's start with a quick look at the Russian Roulette of the business world: investing.

The Throbbing Heart Of Investing: Investors

Picking a stock or other opportunity to invest in is a subtle, highly refined process that is practiced by experts who have been rigorously trained in the art and craft of *Applied Values.* Even if you are not yet a high-rolling investor, you have surely seen these men and women on TV business broadcasts; presenting their "Get Stinking Rich Right After Lunch" seminars; and crowded together with other rich financial folks up on the platform at the *New York Stock Exchange*, vigorously applauding *Blessed Money* at the closing bell.

How did they get there?

Usually this question can be answered in a very few words. *Dad. Harvard Business School. Yale Business School. Wharton. Kellogg. Grandpa Thompson. Grandpa Booth-Wheeler III. Uncle Whitley. Say, what a looker. Is she your wife? By the way, I have the negatives.*

But some are self-made financial geniuses. Let us not forget that anything that can be made, can also be unmade. In this connection, it is humbling to reflect that we are all God's children. This family therefore also includes Charles Ponzi (1882 – 1949), Robert Vesco (1935 – 2007) and Bernie Madoff (b. 1938).

Business School

To all indications, Business School is just like Military School with softer beds, no pushups and above all, no minorities to deal with. Well, there are a few "tokens" – hardly to be considered, as they will all drop out by second semester. Even if they should graduate, they will all work directing non-profits devoted to helping other "tokens" get into Business School. They will never be serious competitors for grandpa's company, so you can pretend to enjoy their loud music, spicy food and funny ways. Hey – it's only until graduation anyway.

There are very few "panty raids" in Business School, so if fetishistic sex is a priority for you, you might be happier in Film School or at the University of Colorado.

- *Hint:* If you actually must enroll in the school, refuse from the outset to do any reading, to write any papers or even to attend any courses. Make it clear to the faculty and administration that such activities are always relegated to Staff anyway. You have better things to do with your time, such as learning to mix an excellent (or dreadful) martini (see *Chapter One).*

Getting Real With Real Estate

Investors are frequently reminded of the traditional security of investing in real estate. After all, as the cliché goes, "God isn't making any more land."

Clearly anyone who repeats this dreary cliché is taking a chance on becoming a Landing Zone for Thunderbolts, arrogantly claiming to know what God may or may not be doing. What hubris! Maybe God *is* making more land, or quietly improving previously unappealing tracts at Cape Inexpensive, Arkansas. Or moving *Buddy & Lester's Double-Wide City* to better locations through a series of earthquakes and tsunamis. Even if He isn't doing that, maybe He's working on something else for His creatures to invest in.

But absent Theological Certainty, there is still a widespread notion that it's good to own something solid, something that can be taken from you only with difficulty, something in which the buyer can "build equity."

This situation lends itself beautifully to exploitation by anyone seeking to fail. The supposedly "failure proof" nature of the business makes it even more stunningly spectacular when the *Failure Aspirant* manages to engineer a dramatic *Real Estate Plummet.* It is always warming for us to welcome another equity-destroying event.

Hint: For *Super Failure* in the *Real Estate* category, convince your investor group to:

- Buy a thriving 500-unit Palm Beach luxury hotel with two golf courses, and convert it into a bebop jazz club with free lodging for musicians who are recovering from heroin addiction.

- Convert the golf courses into ecologically "green" habitats for herons and snail darters. Stage events with free food and drink for the community during *Brotherhood Week.*

- Purchase and demolish a 10-square-block lot in downtown Dallas and construct a rent-free community for unwed illegal immigrant mothers from Uganda; unengaged fathers from Samoa; and un-fraternity-pinned grandmothers from Keego Harbor, MI 48033.

- Provide liquor, free steak and booths to recruit new minority Labor Union Members.

Remember, the future belongs to the bold, and this is never more true than when it refers to bold *Super Failures.*

Failure Through Business Bloopers: Making The Ooops! Factor Work For You

Cultivate the habit of making “honest mistakes” and “accidental oversights.” It’s what all the best *International Movers and Shakers* do. That way, when they’re trapped in fiscal or monetary shenanigans, which they always are, their instant spring-loaded reflex is to “deeply regret what was, after all, just an *Honest Mistake.*” Or their lawyer will announce to the world press, “We have every confidence that our client – this world respected financier – will be fully exonerated of any wrongdoing with regard to what was obviously an *Accidental Oversight.*”

In other words,

- Ooops! Now how the heck did *that* happen?

- Golly, that grounder must a just took (*sic*) a tricky hop past my Inner Shortstop.

  Or even,

- Well, for heck's sakes, that intercontinental multi-zillion-dollar transaction must have just slipped through the cracks while I was (a) *Thinking the Great Thoughts*, or (b) So *Deeply Involved* with my charity work, helping chase flies away from all those thin kids in underdeveloped countries on Earth and other nearby planets.

If *Failure Aspirants* work diligently at believing that *Honest Mistakes* and *Accidental Oversights* are perfectly reasonable, that belief will become so deeply ingrained in their natures that no polygraph exam can ever reveal any hint of deliberate wrongdoing.

Money: The Engine Of Finance

It goes without saying that money is the central element of all financial activities. Unless the *Failure Aspirant* learns how to handle money properly, he/she is unlikely ever to understand how to handle it improperly enough to *Plummet.* Let's take a moment to review some basics.

"Successful" people learn to manage money wisely, discovering clever ways for *money to make lots more money* so they and their associates can prosper. Forever. That is, unless Democrats or Socialists or Greenpeace Internationalists control Congress. But clearly, before anyone can manage money wisely, they must have the money to manage. This can be tricky, but the truly motivated usually manage to acquire a bundle.

There are several major roads to this acquisition:

- *Inheritance (by far the best, most reliable and painless route)*
- *Finding it in an empty lot or in an abandoned Ford Ranger pickup (not a 100% reliable business plan)*
- *Suing someone for whiplash, plagiarism, sexual harassment, etc.*
- *Winning it by gambling, including lotteries*
- *Stealing it (legally or illegally)*
- *Working for it*
- *Investing in sexual enhancement drugs*
- *Investing in other drugs (legal or illegal)*
- *Creating, having or doing something others are willing to pay for (legal or illegal)*

In a word, as the *Ancient Wisdom* would have it – Buy low, sell high. In the case of *Failure Aspirants,* the reverse is to be followed. And while you're at it, make sure you unbalance your budget and check book. Some day you will thank us for this advice.

So the revised, enlightened formula for *Super Failure at Finance* becomes:

Buy high, sell low !

Failure Through Bold, Suicidal Entrepreneurism

Few financial techniques in the world can *Plummet* you to *Catastrophic Comprehensive Failure* (including, but not limited to, long jail sentences and bodily harm) than losing the money of humorless people who do not see the strategic and philosophical value of *Losing Huge Quantities of Money.*

One way to guarantee making enemies and losing money is to become *General Partner* in an investment group that puts clients' money in a common stock portfolio consisting of (for example):

- *A chain of penis reduction clinics*
- *Used food kiosks*
- *Sicilian nose oil futures*
- *Camouflage toothpaste for hygiene-conscious Idaho militiamen*
- *Van Gogh/ Picasso/ Modigliani print paper towels*
- *A musical comedy based on the life of Warren G. Harding*
- *Franchise baby back rib restaurants in Saudi Arabia*

- *Sun dried sushi vending machines*
- *Submarine cruises (L.A. – Vladivostok; N.Y. – Capetown (half-hour port calls in Caracas, Tenerife, Tristan da Cunha)*
- *A retirement community group: Lean-To City; Ancient of Days Village; Last Stop – All Out Manor*
- *Wholesale previously owned underwear outlet*

There are as many possibilities are there are nightmare scenarios! Dare to dream of catastrophes that involve *Mergers, Acquisitions* and other *Devastating Losses!*

Hint: *Undue Diligence* saves lots of time. Why bother examining all those pesky papers and dealing with dreary lawyers and CPAs, when you can simply sign on the dotted line?

CHAPTER THREE POINT FIVE

FAILURE IN RADIO AND TELEVISION

We decided to make this a half-chapter, since it contains elements from both Chapter Three (*Failure in Business and Finance*) and Chapter Four, which follows (*Failure in the Arts*). Broadcasting is serious business; but it is often involved with aspects of the arts.

It behooves the serious F*ailure Apsirant* to understand this critical category crossover, which offers the possibility of a rare *Double Plummet!*

The 20th Century ushered in the Age of Broadcasting. First radio, then television, interconnected all of America ... and ultimately the entire world. More intimate, more flexible and more immediate than newspapers and magazines ("print media"), the "live media" of broadcasting swept the nation, not only as provider of news and entertainment, but also as the handmaiden of advertising (the "business" part of the equation).

More impactful than movies, because of their real-time excitement, radio and TV became our nation's dominant reality, the campfire around which we huddled day and night, night and day, morning and afternoon, prime time and late night, to discover and rediscover who we are, what we think ... and who our heroes are.

Losing It On The Air

Until the internet exploded with its endless chat rooms and handheld toys, TV was the overwhelming fact of American life. It was the star-maker, the storyteller, the greatest sales tool that ever existed. And it still is, to a great degree.

In Buck Henry's brilliant dark comedy *To Die For,* a teenage girl expresses the pointlessness of doing anything unless it's on TV. This may be the single most succinct statement ever made about the real American Dream.

Its inherent, undisputed greatness makes television a simply ideal category for the *Failure Aspirant.* The enterprising *Loser* can *Plummet* in two interpenetrating dimensions of broadcasting:

- Programming choices (content and format)
- Behavior of on-air personnel

Let's take a closer look.

Failure Due To Programming Choices

Here are some suggestions for TV program directors keen on dramatic *Failure.* Sure-fire ratings-killers include such fare as:

- *Tony! Tony! Tony!* Finally – an all Tony Danza format! Nonstop 24/7 programming of the adorable ex-boxer acting ex-adorably.

- *The Test Pattern Channel.* "Best of the Tests" features geometrical patterns from TV stations nationwide, even from foreign countries with funny names and weird writing!

- *Retro TV.* Not content to simply re-run old black and white shows, this channel actually *de-colorizes* new material so it appears in several shades of grey, darker grey and extremely dark grey.

- *Celebrity Ironing.* Reality shows like "Hollywood Household Help" (maids and gardeners tending the mansions of the mighty); "Beverly Hills Pool Boys"; "Recycling & Waste Management of the Stars." The insider's inside view of famous people's bathrooms, utility closets and tool sheds.

- *The Chess Channel.* Current and classic matches of the world's greatest International Grand Masters huddling hour after hour, pondering their positions. Viewers learn the subtleties of the *Nimzo-Indian Defense*, the Blackburne Gambit – hell, why stop there? Delve into the *Barnes Defense ("Fried Fox" Variation)*!

- *Don't Fish – Cut Bait!* Designed for the *Compleat Indoorsman* who loves bait, but dislikes bobbing all day in a boat, occasionally hooking and suffocating ugly scaly creatures. Host shows many ways to chop worms, killies, chum and squishy insects.

- *The Telethon Channel.* Inexhaustible 2nd and 3rd rate performers donate their talents on behalf of lesser-known charities such as *Itchy Scalp Relief; Paraguayan Dungeon Reform*; *The Gen. William Westmoreland Home for Retired Snipers*; *United Methodists for Buddha; Mittens for the Hearing Impaired*; *The Jerry Vale Library*; *Bibles for Belarus*; etc.

Failure On Radio

Radio executives also have some fine opportunities to go bust. Radio is often called "the theatre of the mind," since listeners must visualize what is happening.

The absence of pictures forces the audience to indulge their imaginations, and project meaning into what they hear. Since most current radio programming is neither drama nor comedy, as in the old days, this leaves listeners in the uncomfortable position of having to make "theatre" out of (a) endlessly dopey pop, rock or gangsta rap programs, or (b) endlessly dopey talk shows based on other listeners telephoning the host with their uninformed, bigoted and fumferingly expressed opinions.

This offers fine opportunities for the *Failure Apsirant* to provide radio programming to enhance his chances of *Plummeting.* Just a few examples of shows that offer outstanding opportunities for ratings catastrophes:

- *Great Documents of American History.* Elderly Professors Emeritus from fancy Eastern universities read, word for word, all 85 *Federalist Papers* by Alexander Hamilton, James Madison and John Jay. This show, by popular demand or not, is repeated every weekend until the station is sold to a media conglomerate from North Korea, who will switch instantly to a combined Tae Kwon Do and Kim Chee Recipe format.

- *Here, Doggie, Doggie.* Aimed at dog lovers everywhere – and who isn't? – this show presents an interminable series of barking marathons, in which the most leather-lunged pooches win scholarships to dog training academies, where they learn to control their barking reflex.

- *What's My Minority?* Individuals of diverse backgrounds speak for several minutes with the host. Listeners call in to win insignificant prizes* by correctly identifying the backgrounds of those individuals. Without their eyes to help, the audience is forced into the "theatre of the mind" where tiny clues help them discern the origin of the Mystery Minority. Recent minorities that stumped listeners: *Albino Nicaraguan Lesbian; Oklahoman Cyclops* (from Enid); and surprisingly, *Nicolas Sarkozy, President of France,* who was mistaken for a Canadian disc jockey.

- *Speech Impediment Du Jour.* An hour in prime time. The format speaks for itself; guest stutterers, victims of bilateral sibilants, baby talkers – all get their 15 minutes of fame, even if it does take them 60 minutes to get through their quarter hour.

* NOTE: *Awarding really unimportant prizes will help de-popularize the show. We recommend items such as: a day's supply of baby wipes; a left-handed can opener; an 8-track tape of Don Ho's Greatest Hits; one ticket to the Ice Capades, etc.*

Failure Due To On-Air Behavior

Clearly any behavior that is considered universally obnoxious (see other chapters) can also be employed to help you fail on the air. Indeed, the vaster the audience, the greater the opportunities for offending. Due to space considerations, we offer here only a few of the more successful approaches:

- Attack the most precious personal beliefs of your listeners. For example, tell them that God couldn't possibly exist because He would never create anyone as repulsive and stupid as your listeners. Challenge Him to strike the station's antenna with a lightning bolt to prove He is there. Proclaim that motherhood is a foolish waste of time, and encourage your audience to scorn, mock and deride their mothers and grandmothers in public.

- Insist that all baseball playoffs, beauty pageants and quiz shows are fixed. (This may, in fact, be true – but the idea is upsetting to the public anyway.)

- Announce that a local restaurant is giving away free dinners to the first thousand people who show up. Also, every car dealer in town has agreed to give a free car to the first ten totally naked people who come to the showroom.

- Scold listeners for being unintelligent and uneducated. Taunt them with quotes in Latin and Sanskrit, and obscure references to Medieval Norse literature.

- Do an entire half hour segment entirely in Morse Code.

- Defy the audience to switch the dial to another station and keep it there forever.

- Urge listeners to take the radio into the bathtub with them. This should work only once per listener who follows the instruction.

- Produce a "nostalgia" program of old-time silent movies. All the listeners will hear is the clattering of the 16mm projector and your occasional howls of laughter at Mack Sennett one-reelers.

Remember – as in other categories, the only limits to your *Failure* are in your own failed imagination!

CHAPTER FOUR

FAILURE IN THE ARTS
by
Kath-Tharynne
Performance Director
Church of Our Lady of the Footlights

Serial Failure *Kath-Tharynne (she uses only her hyphenated first name to spare loved ones embarrassment) began her performing career in a 3rd Grade spelling bee, correctly spelling the word "Rump. R-U-M-P. Will someone please touch my exposed rump?*

Rump." Her vivid "show and tell" performance caused problems for shocked parents and teachers. But she enjoyed the attention and was off on her chosen path. "Performing is not a job," she has always insisted. "It's a calling. In my case, it's actually more like a screaming." Expelled from a series of elementary and middle schools, Kath-Tharynne turned to Street Theatre for self-expression. Failing at Street Theatre, in rapid succession she attempted Avenue Theatre, Boulevard Theatre and finally – desperate for income – Freeway Interchange Theatre.

Sadly, due to the speed of the passing audiences, her performances of theatrical classics remained underappreciated. Finally she reverted to her 3rd Grade triumph, reducing her one-woman versions of A Streetcar Named Desire *and* The Cherry Orchard *to simply flashing her rump at speeding motorists. Upon release from prison she founded the non-conformist religious institution-showcase,* Church of Our Lady of the Footlights. *She has graciously agreed to contribute these pages. – The Editors*

About Acting

Acting is among the most ancient of human activities. Since time immemorial, men and women have felt the urge to express for their fellow creatures the subtle truths of humanity's inner life.

In modern times, updating that prehistoric urge, contemporary actors in a million restaurants worldwide are expressing for their fellow creatures the subtle truths of

Today's Specials!!!

- *Quiche and Radicchio Salad*
- *Seared Tuna Topped with Blazing Goat Cheese*
- *Lemon Grass Panini*
- *Saddle of Unborn Tofu au Gratin*

The "Tableside Proscenium" has historically provided indispensable training for actors as they progress through the required stages of their artistic development, which tend to follow this progression:

- Extra on a *Movie of the Week* ("That's me handing the newspaper to the guy standing behind the zookeeper!").

- Three carefully-rehearsed lines in a suburban Community Theatre production of *Death of a Salesman*, adapted and directed by a talented suburban realtor.

- A gritty performance in a local cable TV commercial for *Lucille's Bedspreads & Notions* ("Lucille just *won't* be undersold. Word!").

- Second lead in a "pilot" for *HBO* or *Showtime* ("A street-wise cop discovers he's an alien.").

- A hilarious recurring role as the non-Armenian-speaking cleaning lady/man (Rosalita/Federico) on an *Armenian Teletime* sitcom.

Gradually, as actors study and gain hands-on experience in the theatre, they qualify for roles as diversified as *A Guard; Third Laundress; Blind Woman With Tray; Second Gondolier; Twisted Corpse; Peeling Tree Near Stream* and eventually, if all goes according to their hopes and dreams, *Hamlet, Prince of Denmark* ... or *Hedda Gabler.*

The problem is that 99% of the time, all does *not* go according to the actors' hopes and dreams. In fact, very little goes anywhere near their hopes and dreams. Some other guy gets to embody *Hamlet;* some other girl will immortalize *Hedda.* And that's the way it *really* goes.

This situation is painful and frustrating to actors, who are in most respects very like other human beings. They want to succeed in their chosen profession. They want to express the subtle truths of humanity's inner life. They want to earn a living. They want to be appreciated and loved and admired and hounded for autographs in wildly expensive exclusive restaurants where they no longer have to express the subtleties of *Today's Specials.* Now they just eat those *Specials* and overtip.

Obviously living that dream is nearly always impossible, due to the nature of the business. And yet, the virtual certainty of endless rejection offers a golden opportunity for actors to embrace blessed *Failure* – if they can but learn to *Plummet* !

Actors: It's Never Too Early To Fail

Any budding thespian who is tuned in to the subtle truths of humanity's inner life will quickly recognize that the real world's truth is humanity's *outer* life. After all, that's where other people are – including the people who will pay you to act, or more probably, will *not* pay you to act.

There is a tragic misunderstanding about "training" or "studying." Most aspiring actors assume that, because they took driving lessons that led to a driver's license; took tennis lessons and learned to play tennis; studied French and learned to order a *Steak Frites* – that they can learn to act by studying "acting."

This delusion is common to people who believe that *anyone* can "learn" an art by "taking classes" in that art. Wrong. When it comes to the arts, unless you already "get it" you will never "*be it.*" People with no rhythm can't learn dancing – they can only learn to mimic *dance steps.* Similarly, if you aren't already good at making believe you're someone else, you can never "learn" to be a good – let alone great – actor. You can only learn to move around onstage saying memorized words and trying not to bump into anything that will hurt you, while making the audience gasp and laugh.

But that doesn't stop stagestruck men and women from seeking out respected drama coaches and auditioning for their classes. (Do you have to audition for a typing class? For woodworking or scuba diving? *Clue.)* For every talented aspirant there are dozens, probably hundreds, of poor clunkers whose time would be better spent working on *Failure Techniques,* to hasten their mastery of *Plummeting* – which *can* be learned by one and all, regardless of natural talent!

And of those aspiring performers accepted by the great gurus, only a dinky fraction of the most talented will develop into fine actors. Further, of those who develop into fine actors, an even dinkier fraction will ever have a satisfying career acting. Not only will they usually not be hired, but will constantly suffer the frustration of watching untalented doofuses earn fame and fortune using talents totally unrelated to the theatre.

Failing Your Casting Call

All acting hopefuls, young and old alike – even successful ones – have to submit to the humiliation of casting calls (sometimes called "cattle calls") until they win a number of *Golden Globe* or *Tony* or *Critics' Choice* awards. At that point, producers come looking for them, not the other way around. Once an actor credibly inhabits the stratosphere called *Stardom*, there are no more auditions. Only phone calls or text messages among agents, producers, casting directors (and sometimes offshore bankers).

Luckily, most of us, talent aside, will never whiff the rarified air of that stratosphere. We can go directly to well-deserved oblivion! That said, it may happen that the Gentle Reader may find him/herself at an audition along with fellow actors. You have an advantage, however, not only in your certainty of your impending rejection, but (if you have learned from this book) you also have the tools necessary to make that rejection all the swifter and more bitter!

CASE HISTORY:
Sample Casting Call Rejection Inducers

Loser's Guide graduates have *Plummeted* dramatically by using these lines in casting calls. You may, of course, vary them to suit your own situation.

- *I will now translate my sides into Swedish – the only civilized language for a film.*
- *Anyone got any good dope? It helps me with my Inner Work.*
- *Which of you [guys/gals] do I have to have sex with to get this part? Or is it* all *of you?*
- *Say, what if instead of a cop, my character is a talking sea otter?*
- *How dare* you *give* me *a line reading? Don't you know I studied with Dirk Dark back in Poughkeepsie?*

Sometimes it's not so much what you say, but how you look and what you do that will guarantee a quick (and maybe permanent) exit from the world of casting calls. Try any of these tactics:

- *Wear garments made of any shiny waxlike substance.*
- *Bring your pet [ferret, chimp, tropical fish, macaw, llama] along.*
- *Arrive costumed as an Oscar.*

- *Have a sinister hulking bodyguard prowl scowlingly around the room while you audition. [Option: he can make rude gestures to the casting panel.]*
- *Enter with a large bloody carcass wrapped in butcher's paper, place it on chair near you while you read.*

Failure At Humor

If there is one tragedy about comedy, it's this:

Everybody thinks they have a great sense of humor.

Almost all of them are dead wrong.

Yet, most people will sooner admit to any other fault than humorlessness. They will cheerfully cop to being bad at math; not knowing sports; being color blind; having a sexually transmitted disease; losing badly at chess; not being fashionable dressers. They will agree, smilingly, that they have no head for business; no talent for music; can't draw to save their souls. Throwing their hands heavenward, they will proudly acknowledge to the universe that they are hopeless in the kitchen – can barely boil bread or bake a salad. But don't you *dare* hint that they may be tone-deaf when it comes to humor.

That's where most people draw the line.

At one time or another, you're surely heard someone insist, "I have as good a sense of humor as the next guy – but *that's just not funny!*"

It gets worse. Very often, people who really don't get it, thinking they *do* get it, can't resist trying to be funny. And if there's one thing that is guaranteed to kill humor in the egg, it's trying too hard. This is particularly painful to watch when wannabe "comedians" are going through their routines and "dying." The less the audience laughs, the more frantically they try. They trot out the nasty words. They show their rumps.

[*See Introductory Sketch at the beginning of this chapter. – The Editors*].

They resort to insulting the audience. Only a few comedians have succeeded with that approach, and then only because there was also something really true and funny behind their insults. By definition, unless you are already funny, your insults can never be funny. They can only be insulting – offensive, gratuitous and may result in unwelcome visitors later in the dressing room. Or on your way outside to your car – you know, the one with the smashed windshield and flattened tires.

Good News For Losers

The above commentary offers the *Failure Aspirant* an excellent blueprint for *Plummeting* in the category *Humor,* and its less intelligent sub-set, *Comedy.* Simply re-read the above paragraphs, and the path will be amply clear. In order to *Plummet* in humor, simply:

- Believe – albeit mistakenly – that you're a really really really hilarious person, every bit the equal of Robin Williams, Lily Tomlin, Jay Leno, Richard Pryor, Gracie Allen or other comedians you admire.

- Copy your role model's basic approach, slugging in your own tepid (or preferably, gelid) material.

- Go to the next "open mike" in your city's most popular comedy club, which will surely be called *Chuckie's Chuckle City, The Belly Laff, Ye Olde Yok Factorie* or some other name that tries too hard. It is always a good first step toward *Failure* when the owner of a comedy club clearly has no sense of humor, and is trying too hard!

- Put your name on the talent list. When the emcee introduces you, grab the mike and aggressively begin your act.

- No matter what the audience does, for better or worse, keep plowing straight ahead with your jokes, songs, stories or insults.

- Become abusive if necessary (see above comment on insults). If the management tries to interrupt you, fight back. This will enhance your chances of negative press coverage. But remember the old dictum – it doesn't matter what they write about you, as long as they write about you.

- The more quickly you develop a reputation as "the comedian who just *isn't funny,*" the more quickly you are likely to be relegated to your proper place at the bottom of the heap!

CASE HISTORY:
Choosing A Simply Awful Professional Name

More good news. Choosing an annoying stage name can help speed you into unpopularity, and precipitate the destruction of your career! But be careful: make sure you are not accidentally witty or inventive. Otherwise, the ploy might backfire, as it did for "Whoopi Goldberg," who became a major comedy star despite her calculatedly obnoxious alias.

We know. The overwhelming likelihood is that you are not even *remotely* as funny as Whoopi is. We will take that on faith, and move confidently forward to the process of creating an annoying stage name. When we select one, we might also consider, as Whoopi did, deliberately mis-spelling it (Whoopi should be spelled "Whoopee!") to add to the fun.

Observe that the formula that produced "Whoopi Goldberg" is the following:

Joyous Outcry + Jewish Surname = Successful Alias.

Let's try our hand with it.

- Yippee Epstein (Yip Pee Epstein)
- Yahoo Feldman (Yah Who? Feldman)
- Ha Ha Ha Wexler (Ja Ja Ja Wexler)

There are all good choices as obnoxious stage names. But here the Gentle Reader may well ask: Hey, what about me? I live in (Idaho, Mississippi, American Samoa). Using a Jewish name, even as a blatantly tasteless joke, may be so unacceptable to the locals as to keep me from even getting on stage to bomb in public! This would indeed be a setback, because it is impossible to enjoy the full measure of *Failure at Humor* without enduring lots of booing and flying fruit, vegetables and preferably eggs as well.

No problema. We simply re-juggle the proposition with another formula:

Non-Ethnic Joyous American Outcry + 100% Real American Patriot Non-Jewish Surname = Successful Alias.

Examples:

- Hot Dang! Tompkins
- Oh, Youuuuu Betcha Swenson
- Wal, I Swan Gibbs

At some point it may be necessary, just to get on and off stage with kneecaps intact, to adopt an Italian stage name. We suggest something like:

- Hip-Hip-Hooray Bartolini
- Hoo-Hah Santucci
- Yes! Yes! Yessss! Di Giovanni
- Boy Oh Boy! La Rocca

Arrogance is a popular currency in Hollywood and on Broadway. In a profession that is driven by massive ego-power, only thick-skinned and aggressive individuals get to play with the "movers and shakers." Want a career? Start moving and shaking, my friend.

Bonus hint:

- *Act as your own agent.* No big time talent agent wants to handle you unless you're already a big star anyway. So go for it. Choose a powerful Hollywood-sounding Super Agent name like Darryl De Satan or Sid Morty. Set up meetings with producers (or more likely, with their underlings).

- Whcn you walk in, introduce yourself by both names, as both agent and "talent." The producer (or underling) won't care, since he has no intention of hiring you under any circumstances. He already knows all the agents and actors he needs to know. His Rolodex and iPhone speed-dial are already filled to overflowing.

You're already on your way down!

Failure At Painting And Sculpture

So much criticism has been leveled at the world of the plastic arts as to make it nearly pointless to comment further in these pages. Suffice to say that in recent decades, schmeering almost any gooey substance onto almost any surface – with almost any degree of competence or preferably, incompetence – can result in a successful career for the schmeerer and his/her inner circle.

The same goes for people who weld pieces of useless metal to other pieces of useless metal, thereby producing even larger pieces of useless metal. (Sometimes bright colors are involved.) If the resulting larger piece of useless metal is then given an inspirational title such as "Yearning For Uzbekistan," "How Madeleine Soothed Me," "Cradle Cramps," "Only Epstein Really Knew," etc., then it is considered *High Art.* This means that eager but tasteless zillionaires, or (more likely still) tasteless City Councils that are starved for municipal lawn sculpture that proves their commitment to the Arts, will buy them for huge fees and plant them in public areas, where birds of many species can foul the useless metal with useful fertilizer.

We therefore encourage the *Failure Aspirant* to learn to (a) Find useless pieces of metal; and (b) Learn to weld. One of two results is then likely. (1) You will become unimaginably rich for doing nothing more difficult than lighting a hot flame and shielding your eyes from it; or (2) You will fail miserably at creating "art." Either way, you win.

Minimalist "art" is a brilliantly inventive hoax we can all use to advantage. Example: in music, one note, chord or phrase played over and over can be acclaimed as an ingenious "musical breakthrough." A block of stone with one chip removed is a "statue." Get it? A clump of steel stuck in cement can be titled "Hope" when you exhibit it in Philadelphia – and a day later re-titled "Despair" in Detroit. The work will very likely receive rave reviews for "honesty" and "relevance" in both venues.

"Primitive Art" – Shame Or Disgrace?

If you are particularly enterprising, you can find, make or assemble from almost anything found in an alleyway or urban gutter, any number of "art works" to promote as "primitive art." The following pages are a cautionary essay by one of those know-it-all wise guys who claims to see through our plan for *Failure in the Arts,* obviously wishing to thwart our mission. Bad cess to him.

That said, it is crucial to know that such Gloomy Gus spoil-sports are out there. Reality and awareness must always be our guides.

CASE HISTORY:
A Dissenting Opinion That Pisses Us Off

"PRIMITIVE ART" ? – Puh-LEEEEZE!

Unfashionable Opinion by
[Name withheld to protect the loathsome person who dared to write this piece of trash]

"When I hear the word 'culture' I reach for my gun," is a quip incorrectly attributed to that witty wag Joseph Goebbels. It is history's only known Nazi punch line, from a play by Nazi Poet Laureate Hanns Johst (1890-1978). I can only suppose that the author must have been thinking about primitive culture when he said that.

After all, primitive culture – particularly primitive "art" – is simply too awful to be taken seriously, even by non-Nazis. Yet millions of people are regularly hoodwinked by primitive gobbledygook. They read about it. They discuss it. They buy it. They even hang it on their own walls, where people who know them can see it!

There's altogether too much of this "primitive art" around, masquerading as real art. It's time to fight back. Here I intend to strike a blow for artistic integrity with a realistic reflection upon the pathetic emptiness of "primitive art" – despite the shrill protestations sure to come from its Politically Correct fans.

By Their Fruits Shall Ye Know Them

Primitive peoples still exist on Earth. Indeed there are far more backward societies than even anthropologists may wish to admit. But there's no such thing as a primitive civilization; that's a contradiction in terms. Undeveloped people may have tribal groupings or even rudimentary societies, never civilizations.

That's because a "civilization" is by definition an evolved society that has developed an urbanized life with civic services such as sanitation, health care and education. A civilization is literate, with widespread knowledge of science, technology, statecraft and indoor plumbing. It has architecture, agriculture and dry cleaning. Civilized people use credit cards, room service and fax machines. They fly in airplanes and know how to parallel park. A civilization has a rich intellectual life and the ongoing group awareness we call "recorded history." Most germane to this essay, civilizations produce highly refined arts. Any society lacking the abovementioned attributes – especially the arts – is not a "civilization." It's just a bunch of folks.

Primitive people have only a sketchy grasp of abstractions, and little ability to convert abstractions into anything useful. So they remain becalmed among their roots and berries, their backwoods mutilation rituals, their gawking masks and fearsome mud-gods. The poor creatures slumber on in ignorance and superstition.

They live in poverty and illness, swallowed up by flies and by fear; helpless pawns of blind circumstance. They are incapable of improving their lives because they don't have the physical, mental or social tools necessary for advancing into civilization. They live in an endless summer camp for underachievers.

Art ... Or Stuff?

Because they are not civilized, primitive people do not make art, they make stuff. They don't have the understanding or the skills required to create real art. Perhaps they feel the urge to express themselves. But express what? What on earth do savages have to express that could possibly interest anyone but another savage? The content of our expression is what we know and feel. What do primitives know and feel? Ignorance, fear, helplessness and the need to go potty. That's what primitives have to express, and because they themselves are so unformed and so uninformed, their self-expression inevitably emerges as clunky statues, misshapen mud things, grotesque masks or monotonous chants and log-whacking. Primitive culture isn't in fact "culture" at all – it's only behavior.

Any civilized person who is not taste-impaired or in denial will recognize primitives' diddlings for what they are: Primordial attempts at art. Repeat, attempts. But they are not art any more than lobbing yak poo at a bird's nest is NBA-level basketball.

Still, some civilized people actually claim to like this gack! Of course most of them are simply lying. Their fondness for "primitive art" isn't based on artistic criteria; it's a political statement. It's wishful thinking at its most dishonest: they so desperately want savages to be better than they really are, that they are willing to pretend that the savages' art is better than it really is! These warmhearted fellows claim to believe that anything created by any person (no matter how unskillful) is "art."

Thus the merest stone age construct or artifact—simply because it resulted from human effort—is a cultural achievement to rival Beethoven's *Eroica*, Van Gogh's *Starry Night* or the glorious Chartres Cathedral.

To them I say, poppycock! I say it louder, in boldface, **poppycock!** The spewings and doings of brutes, no matter how sincerely they may reflect primitive terror, confusion or fertility fun, are not "art" or "literature" or "music" any more than the barking of hyenas or the ribbiting of tree frogs are sonnets or sonatas. They are silly, incompetent trifles that ought to evoke honest pity, perhaps even derision, but certainly not praise.

Real Art Isn't Easy

The queer notion that any self-expression is art; that artistic genius resides in every human is simply dead wrong. Fine art is a great miracle, achieved only rarely and with great difficulty. Some artists are more sensitive, more imaginative, better educated, harder working and more skillful than others; therefore some art is better than other art. Civilized art is better than primitive art because civilization provides a better cultural environment for creating fine art than does the rainforest.

Few would deny the "natural human impulse" to make art. But when fine art results from that "natural human impulse," it is in fact the very opposite of "natural." There is nothing automatic about art. Art is the deliberate, intelligent reworking of reality. Art is artifice, designed to add to and thereby surpass ordinary reality. It improves upon the natural to create something timeless and emblematic. Art defies death by overcoming the merely natural; it connects all humankind by tapping into subtle essences underlying apparent differences. Thus it bridges the centuries. "Primitive art" is lucky to bridge the next shrub.

Cultural Denial Is Still Denial

Still, primitivo-philiacs pay big bucks for homely statues or clumsy clay pots that might fetch mild praise for an eager pre-schooler. Sophisticated urbanites who really ought to know better ooh-and- aah over root-mash splashed on hemp; over low-fidelity wire-recordings of savannah grunting; over bad indigenous weaving badly dyed. "It's so deliciously ... primitive!" they gush, spreading more *pesto brie* onto their stone ground multi-grain crackers.

Here's a simple reality check for "primitive art" buyers: would they demand a refund if, through some mixup, their "primitive masterwork from India" turned out instead to be the work of a 7-year-old from Indiana? If so, then their decision to buy the piece was political, maybe even financial – but certainly not an artistic decision. Otherwise they'd keep it and still consider their money well spent.

Relativism has no place in art. There's a limit to how much we can "grade on a curve." The unadorned fact is that in the real world some things – including art – are better than other things. The more we educate our taste, the less easily we can be fooled. Civilized people learn to distinguish the authentic from the counterfeit, the superior from the inferior. They ought to be honest enough to admit that "primitive art" is a baby step for people bumbling through social and artistic toddlerhood.

Does this mean that "primitive art" is worthless? Of course not. It is occasionally moving, charming, even instructive – just as a baby's finger paintings or mud pies can move or amuse indulgent, loving parents. But that does not mean that it should be ranked with the evolved, civilized art born of educated sensibilities working with determination and discipline.

The act of nailing a frame around a canvas splattered with paint does not automatically make it "art," much less a masterwork. The mere process of recording sounds does not magically convert those sounds into fine music. Finally, no purchase price is extravagant enough to transform clumsy wood hackings into "statues."

Beauty may be in the eye of the beholder, but if it isn't in the art as well, we're just kidding ourselves.

CHAPTER FIVE

FAILURE AT WRITING
by
Brock Lifter

The name Brock Lifter streaked briefly, then Plummeted *dramatically, across the Literary Firmament in the late 1990s with publication of his much-reviled first (and as inevitably happened, last) novel, the "embarrassingly predictable" mystery,* What the Lithuanian Saw.

Every major film studio disclaimed even hearing of the book. Mr. Lifter's planned visit to the Sundance Film Festival, in hope of making an independent film deal, was thwarted when he was refused boarding on all planes to Park City. His name had suddenly appeared, in pencil, on airline "No Fly" lists as well as "No Ride" lists for bus companies. Few authors can speak with greater authority on what it takes to achieve Failure at Writing. *We are pleased to present Brock Lifter's commentary, transcribed from a series of telephone calls from an undisclosed location or locations. There was much static on the line. – The Editors*

This extensive category of the Arts – *Writing* – deserves an expanded chapter because so many people aspire to be writers. Most of them aspire to be good, or even brilliant, writers – the kind who create literature, deathlessly inspirational poetry, blockbuster hit screenplays.

The present study is intended to guide those prescient enough to wish to be *Failed Writers!*

Let's review the literary landscape.

Most people who hunger to be writers have that ambition simply because they can read and even spell fairly well – especially if they have learned to activate the "Spell Check" function on their word processors. Some type fairly accurately, and can print out what they have typed. This encourages them. What emerges from the printer looks just like real "writing" because it has been printed out in black and white, in a legitimate typeface.

Most of these wannabe writers have read books and magazines, and they also know that scripts for movies and TV are "written by" someone. Most exciting to them, some of those "someones" make a fortune writing best sellers or blockbuster movies or hit new TV series and get invited to appear on talk shows. They are invited to dine at exclusive restaurants and sometimes get to flirt with beautiful people who otherwise would never even look twice at them. Maybe not even once.

This convinces many would-be authors that they, too, have a great future in writing. But luckily for the literary world, they don't. And why should they?

Think about it. Not everyone who enjoys food feels obliged to become a chef. Enthusiastic air travelers rarely believe they are born pilots. Few sports fans – even experts on their games – could capably coach children, let alone a professional team.

- *Q: So then why do so many unqualified wannabe's want to be writers?*
- *A: Because in their secret hearts, they just* know *that they have a great book or movie script in them.*

Their secret hearts, of course, are *dead wrong.* Almost nobody has a great book or movie script in them, and that goes for most good professional writers. But this is no time for reality – got to boot up my laptop, pour a drink and ... *create.* Hey, just look at all those overstuffed shelves down at the discount book store. With that much stuff in print, there's surely nothing to it!

CASE HISTORY:
Sample Bad Opening Lines

We all learn in Freshman English (or earlier, if we are unfortunate enough to have spent childhood years in a good school system) of the importance of "seizing" the reader's attention with a powerful opening sentence – one that sets the tone and establishes the context for whatever is to follow. If you can manage a simply dreadful opening line, you greatly improve your chances for *Failure at Writing.*

Recent *Loser's Guide* alumni got rejection slips by Express Return Mail for the following lines. See if you can create any openings that sink to this level of *Plummet!*

- *As a boy Nunzio worked for the Mob, sewing live canaries onto the lips of squealers.*

- *Big Eduardo never masturbated to climax because of his problem with Commitment.*

- *Owen T. Presbie owned a schnauzer called Yank who looked just like Wanda Landowska, but with a slightly more attractive snout.*

- *It's not easy being the only kid on your block from Mars.*

- *"I love the feel of my bullets splattering into your chest," shrieked Gladine as she emptied her Thurmley-Spahn .357 into Clark's shuddering torso.*

- *As a boy, Dirk's imaginary playmate was Queen Victoria.*

- *Big Naomi's eyes were as empty as the Garment District on Yom Kippur; as haunting as a men's room with no Muzak(TM).*

Submitting Your Manuscript

OK, you've poured out your heart onto paper. Or onto a disk. Now what?

Real writers learn that the writing itself is the easiest part of getting your book published. If you don't already have a well-placed agent who has lots of clout with publishers, you're fighting a battle that's not just uphill, it's virtually vertical.

Put that verticality to work for you – but in the other direction.

Plummet!

CASE HISTORY:
Super-Failure In The Novel Form

Following is a perfect example of a good idea gone *brilliantly* bad. The authors recognized that they were writing for *an increasingly illiterate audience, with a rapidly decreasing attention span.* Therefore they all sought to "cut to the chase" so readers could have the best of both worlds: the enjoyment of their favorite literary styles ... with the satisfaction of having "finished" a book – at least in the sense of reading through to the last page.

These *Failure Bound* authors boldly wrote books consisting *entirely of last pages* (in a stroke of genius, actually adding numbered last pages)! This literary "variety pack" spanned the most popular literary genres, thereby providing a veritable bookshelf of novels for the audience.

The popular genres are: Gothic, Pornography; Science Fiction; Western; War and Espionage.

THE BOOK OF LAST PAGES
A Compilation Of Conclusions

Book #1:
Bride Of Paragoric
by Dirk Dark [page 877]

... suddenly thrust the legendary silver dagger Thufpitt into Paragoric's meaty belly, jerking it upward and to the left with all her might. The huge assassin-king screamed in surprised rage and pain, clutching at Esmeralda's throat in a panicked attempt to seize the Golden Raccoon statue and bludgeon her with it. His twisted face was horrible to behold. Pulsing bright red arterial blood surged onto the lush palace bedroom rug, draining Paragoric's vitality with each passing second.

"Bitch-fiend," he gasped, flailing desperately at her with one quivering hand. "Think of all we could have had!"

Esmeralda, her shapely maiden-bosom heaving and straining against her silken bodice with heroic effort, broke free of his bloody grasp.

"Never with thee, thou master of evil!" she hissed. Grasping the Golden Raccoon in her graceful, purposeful hands, she brought the heavy metal statue down on Paragoric's sweaty temple, once, once more, again, again, again, then yet again, and another time or two, until long after her captor had ceased to scream, ceased to squirm, ceased to twitch, ceased to breathe, ceased to do anything; just plain ceased, period. Paragoric was now as dead as any evil king ever gets.

A deep satisfaction crept into Esmeralda's whole being; then disgust; then exhaustion; then exhilaration; finally the ecstasy of total release from the sinister spell that had held her for the five long years she had resisted Paragoric. Now the Golden Raccoon was hers, hers alone, with all that that implied. At last someone would rule the Kingdom with Serfkins and Fropkins living side by side in peace. Oh, she would have challenges from the Imperial Guard, from Wizard Kekkonnen, and from Paragoric's three hundred ambitious sons, but those were risks she was willing to take—had to take. For now she was Esmeralda, Virgin Queen of Zarbia, and monarchs must learn to take risks.

"Yes," Queen Esmeralda smiled to herself, "Yes, it has been worth it, blood and all. Quite, quite worth it." She let the Golden Raccoon slip from her fingers onto the glistening marble floor, and turned toward the balcony. Squaring her shoulders in that determined way of hers, she threw open the doors and went forth to greet her cheering people.

THE END

Book #2:
Black Lace Pantylust Weekend
by Vance R. Slint [page 442*]*

... with his throbbing love-log thrashing wildly, uncontrollably, seeking its deepest satisfaction, driven by an erotic need greater than any that Humberto had known in his whole bawdy life, even with Big Naomi, the only woman who had ever exhausted him. But now, Hilda's glistening little honey-purse seemed to be screaming at him through her soaking leather hot-pants, take me, oh, take me NOW!

This was the moment he had been fantasizing about for three years. With a bestial cry he ripped away her wet diaphanous peasant-blouse in one powerful sweep, and Hilda's huge proud hemispheres tumbled free, shimmering seductively in the campfire-light. He gasped at the sight of all that luscious big tanned flesh, her twin lust-towers twitchingly topped by prominently erect café-con-leche guard-posts.

Meanwhile Hilda sighed at the sheer enormousness of him, unable to take her eyes off it. The titanic gargantuosity of his pulsing, insistent man-thing turned her all weak and fluttery. Her whole body quivered and quaked with instant, mindless desire. "Oh, PLUNGE, Humberto," she begged. "Plunge THAT ... plunge that THERE!"

They took each other hungrily, frantically, animalistically. "My angel, my own," cried Humberto as their pelvis-punishing thrusts crescendoed to a shattering, tumultuous, bone-drenching climax, the most devastatingly vivid that either had ever experienced. "Oh yes yes yes YESSSSSSSSSSSSSSSSSSSSSSSS indeedy!" screamed Hilda as her supple spine arched upward at the panoply of bright stars above, as if seeking there a few final drops of love-ambrosia. All around them nature was still. Hilda and

Humberto dropped into an exhausted, peaceful, sated sleep. Tomorrow was another day, the plasterer was coming, and they'd need all the strength they could get.

THE END

Book #3:
Death Crystals Of Zargax Four
by Jack Von Drachma, Jr. [page 288]

... mammoth gleaming battle-galaxy megaskipped a billion light years and materialized in the outer atmosphere of the now-incinerated Zargaxian capital planet Duufaax. It was a defeated, vanquished, utterly devastated planet; their late hated enemy. There were no longer any life readings at all; all traces of DNA had disappeared.

"They must have megafaced all the macroquarks they had," said Captain Xahhhh contemplatively, his trokhorns glarbering with mixed sadness and triumph. "It was their only way out. Galactic suicide. They have escaped us into another dimension."

"But not for long," troiled Princess Arthlmm, a determined look in her deep frath-colored gezorns. "We'll have their bacon, and soon! My staff is tracking them on the scoposcope."

"They tried our patience far too long," whirred Hrrh, the Drandian elf, a barely perceptible twinkle of victory beaming from his/her/their/its eye stalk. "And we duly primitivized them! So what if Yipwif and his consort Thicka did escape for the moment? They'll never again be a force to reckon with in this quadrant of the galaxy."

"But they will bring evil elsewhere. Meanwhile, we have won the peace here—but what a tragic peace it is," rejoined Captain Xahhhh, heaving the Greftaxian version of a sigh. "King Yipwif and The Death Crystals of Zargax-Four are no more. But neither are the Zargaxians themselves, whom they conquered. Pan-galactic war is an ugly thing, Hrrh. Let's try to avoid it in the future."

"If there is a future," said Princess Arthlmm, moving suddenly closer to Xahhhh, as if for protection from the uncertainties that were certain to come.

"Exactly. If there is one," replied Captain Xahhhh, abruptly turning back to the liquid control panel, flaring the main zarkodrive up to maximum. "But for the moment, other galaxies need our help. Let us put sentiment aside, and do what must be done."

Without a sound Hrrh, the Drandian elf, unstuck him/her/them/itself from the glekmer post and floated over to the appropriate duty station for what he/she/they/it knew was coming next: another intricate intergalactic hyperthrust that would take them through time and thought, there-ward into the next adventure.

"Course, Captain?" asked Hrrh.

"Plot a course for 21st-Century Earth," said he, without looking up from the liquid control panel. "It's the time/place that needs us most. I also have a feeling it's where we might find our old nemesis King Yipwif."

Before his voice had finished echoing in the giant control room, the enormous glistening battle-galaxy was halfway there.

THE END

Book #4:
STIRRUPS IN THE SUNSET
by Mack Bobby Lucas [page 319]

... saw that Old Zeke was dead, peacefully dead with his boots off, just the way the old geezer had wanted it all along. By his pillow they found the note he had scrawled with his last strength. Reading it, they could almost hear the old trail-dog's voice:

> *Guess I'm about done fer. Buck, marry that little gal a yers afore she gits away. You'll find the loot in Luke's trunk. He buried it out by the Gibbs place, about a hunnert paces due west a the ole tree. Too bad Luke didn't live ta face a jury, but I guess justice was did with you drillin' him that way, man ta man, face ta face. He had it comin', the durned busterd, pardon my french. See ya up in them clouds, I reckon.*
>
> *Old Zeke*

"He was such a poet," said Miss Belinda, her big blue eyes moist with decent Western tears. Buck unhitched his gun belt, still fragrant with .44 smoke and good honest frontier sweat.

"I reckon so, Miss Belinda," he nodded, ambushed by unfamiliar feelings. He dropped the gunbelt onto Old Zeke's nightstand with a heavy thud, and suddenly needed to look out the window, out across the beckoning purple hills, across the hills he had begun to call his own. He couldn't look at Old Zeke—not yet. He owed the old man too much. He owed him his life more than once in the years they had ridden together.

And now he was gone; all that was left of the old hell-raiser was that used-up, wrinkled carcass all crumpled up in the bunk, with – of all things! – The Holy Bible clutched in those leathery brown hands of his. Why, that old cuss, hiding his rough-hewn cowboy piety behind rude frontier talk all these years!

Suddenly Buck was aware of Miss Belinda at his side; her perfume, the rustling of all those lady things she wore. He turned to her and for a long moment they looked silently into each others' eyes.

"I've been a-thinking, Buck," she started, hesitantly. "Would ... would you consider staying on as ... as foreman? This spread could use a man like you."

Buck's heart secretly leapt with joy. To be near her, to breathe the same cactus-scented wind she breathed, to walk across the same corral she walked across, sidestepping the same mushy wet things she sidestepped—this was surely the happiness that Old Zeke had talked about so often. And now that happiness could be Buck's ... if only he could give up his wandering, his rambling, his constant moving on.

Miss Belinda puckishly interrupted his reverie. "Well? Cat got your tongue? What do you say, Buck?" She was smiling, a mocking yet inviting smile. Buck looked back through the window, out over the distant hills. He thought it over. The Hawkins Gang wouldn't be any trouble any more. Thatcher and his rustlers were behind bars for a long time to come. Big Luke was dead, by Buck's own hand. Old Zeke had even provided a nice wedding present by telling him where the last of the Thompson gold was buried. Was this the time to settle down? Was this the moment to put down roots, and live a decent honest frontier life with a fine woman, maybe some kids, at his side? Buck turned and looked Miss Belinda full in that pretty face of hers. Suddenly he knew.

"Stay? Sure I'll stay," he smiled. He very, very nearly kissed her lovely upturned lips, but he knew it was not quite time. Whoa – not just yet, thought Buck. There's time enough for that sort of thing later on; yup, enough time for romance later on.

THE END

Book #5:
SHRIEK OF BATTLE, SONG OF MOURNING
by Carl Jack Dope [page 299]

... smoking wasteland that only hours earlier had been the gentle rice paddies of Huoc Thui.

Up above Phil's head choppers thrashed and spluttered through humid, gritty air. Some were chasing VC asses back toward Cambodia; others were ferrying wounded GIs out to hospital ships. Those were the lucky ones. They'd have clean sheets and morphine tonight, maybe get to sneak a feel off a Navy nurse. The unlucky ones were already in canvas body bags, scattered among spent artillery shells. Later those poor dudes would be removed to some final place, a place with no bullets, no incoming mortar rounds, no standard issue leeches in the stinking mud that sticks to you and clogs up the candyass clockwork of your M-16. Phil spat on the ground, philosophically. Yeah, for these poor grunts the war was over – and so was everything else. It was so effin' real it was Zen.

Phil gathered up his incendiaries and hooked them back on his web belt. He scrambled to his feet, shouldered his weapon and walked over to where the Lieutenant was checking a map with S/Sgt. Sweeney. Even after what Sweeney had done for him in the foxhole, Phil still didn't like the hardboiled lifer. He was just too effin' smug, the way he flaunted his combat skills and soldierly wisdom. Yeah, Sweeney was a genuine A-hole, Phil mused as he walked. Look how he's sucking up to the Lieutenant, pretending to care where their next patrol was going.

In Phil's opinion, all patrols were going only one place – straight to hell. Just like this war. Just like the whole effin' Army. Just like the U.S. government. Just like the ARVNs and their puppet government. Just like the VC. They were all alike. They were all part of the same big effin' government, as far as Phil could see. After a long year in hell, Phil understood that the world consisted of just two groups. One was Government. He didn't know exactly what you call the other one, but he knew that he was in it, because he sure as shit wasn't part of no government.

Phil hadn't asked for this war, but he was in it, he thought, as he slogged closer to the Lieutenant and Sweeney. They had put him in it. All the "theys." He didn't ask to get shot at, but they shot at him every day, and he shot back at them every day, and he had no idea if he'd ever hit anything except that rusty old Buick up by Phop Thut. He hadn't ever hit any of the thems from any side. And all sides were trying their effin' best to get him killed. It was existentially absurd, and it bugged him a lot.

But he was getting "short" now – so short he could hardly see over his shower shoes in the morning. Less than a month left on this effin' tour. Then back home, yeah, home, but to what? Mary Lou had never written, and Sid said that the GM plant was closing down. Maybe he should just re-up and stay in the Army? Nah, no way, José. Not while the Army was full of jerks like Sweeney and that guy –

Suddenly Phil was looking up at Sweeney, who was shouting frantically for the medics. But his words didn't seem logically connected. Who'd been hit? Now the Lieutenant was in the mud, shooting toward the tree line, over the body bags. He looked scared. Phil thought it was pretty effin' funny that he couldn't feel anything, and everything seemed so effin' unreal. Maybe being shot wasn't real. Maybe nothing was effin' real. Then Phil felt the cold, and noticed that he couldn't hear the choppers any more. With ironic detachment he recalled the absurd deaths of Socrates and Babe Ruth and Albert Camus and knew he wasn't going home.

Phil smiled wryly. "Eff," he said.

THE END

Book #6:
INTERNATIONAL SHADOW WARS
by Geoff J.M.H. Hambledon [page 111]

... as Krakorkin, that wily old spymaster, had been. Now Hughes meandered across his office, sucking on his old briar. He uncovered the map that had been cloaked for so long, even from the Most Secret Senior Eyes in the Service.

It was a map of Indiana! This was an outrage, clearly the work of a sick mind in extremis. The staff exchanged shocked glances but maintained calm. Throats were cleared, eyebrows raised. Even Cavendish, that master of inscrutability, allowed his mouth to part slightly at one corner. Hughes continued slyly. "This is where we'll recommend the military lads launch their nuclear attack."

"But great heavens, Hughes," ejaculated MacLish, "We can't bomb the U.S. – they're our closest allies!"

"That's precisely what the other side expects us to think," chortled Hughes, attending to his dwindling dottle. The aroma of Balkan Sobranie filled the room. Suddenly a blinding light flooded MacLish's conspiracy-sensitive brain. It was clear. It was beyond all controversy. It was too perfect. Hughes himself was the mole!

Why hadn't he seen it sooner? Now it all made perfect sense.

Federmann's crumpled hire-car voucher from East Germany – that had smelled of Sobranie. And the dummy passport that Edgar The Pole had lifted from the body of Krakorkin's hatchet-man. That, too, contained microscopic traces of Sobranie-ash. Wigfield down at the lab had confirmed it. The phone in Krakorkin's den was redolent of that scent as well—although Krakorkin never smoked!

MacLish felt cold sweat trickle under his arms, soaking through to his worsted. He wondered if the realization showed on his face, and whether Hughes was armed. The damage that bloody fool had done all these years! But what brilliance of tradecraft: a black African communist passing all these years as a Yorkshire MP's son! Despite himself, MacLish felt a flush of admiration. What attention to disguise, to accent, to all the details of English upper-class behaviour! Everything about his career had been so carefully planned and executed, down to the business of Miss Templeton and her swooning.

But one simple human vice, Hughes's weakness for Sobranie tobacco, had tumbled the most fiendishly clever penetration in the history of international counter-espionnage!

MacLish exchanged a glance across the table with Genkins, who had evidently just reached the same conclusion. The younger man rose, and he and MacLish flanked Hughes.

"I'm afraid the jig is up, Hughes," said Genkins, a Grachler Zed-6 automatic suddenly appearing in his hand.

"Yes, sir, it would appear you have much to answer for," added MacLish, remembering all the cherry-cheeked lads Hughes had sent off to their doom.

Instantly Hughes understood that he was blown. He had taken that one step too far, there was no undoing it. But it had been a great career and he regretted nothing. He smiled a richly ironic smile and raised his hands high above his head, the smoking pipe still clenched in his faux-irregular teeth. "All good operations must come to an end," he said in that mildly sardonic tone of his. "You'll admit I gave you chappies quite a run for your money."

As if he had just remembered the pipe in his mouth, Hughes casually lowered one hand as if to remove it. Instead he gave the stem a brisk twist, then clamped his teeth brutally down. There was a sharp high popping noise. Instantly MacLish knew what had happened.

"The pipe! Quickly, there, Genkins!" he cried, roughly seizing his Chief's arms. But it was already too late. They heard the hiss of the thylohexachlorazide gas and Hughes's sigh as he inhaled the lethal fumes. He was nerve-dead before he hit the table. The others scattered to avoid the deadly effect. Thurston smashed open a window. Hughes, the mole, the man who had betrayed them, was dead in mid-smile. Commonwealth security was seriously compromised, and it would surely take decades to repair the damage.

MacLish looked over at his old partner Genkins. He looked at them all. “It looks as if we’ve got some work ahead of us, lads,” he said. “But let’s do try to keep this on the quiet side, shall we?” Genkins nodded. They all nodded. Then they covered Hughes’s corpse with the big strategic map of Indiana. To a man, they stiffened their upper lips. Thurston rang, and Miss Dickworth brought in some tea. As the rain began again outside, they set about the business of rebuilding their Service. It was the British way.

THE END

CASE HISTORY:
Failure At Hard-Boiled Dick Pulp Fiction

The “hard boiled dick” is a special category of serial detective fiction writing that flourished in American pulp monthlies for nearly a century. Following is a sample installment that spelled "The End" for its author. It was too hard-boiled and too cute to live. There was no 18th Installment for McTack John Hardee, who *Plummeted* out of the world of hard-boiled dick fiction. Changing his pen name to Clarissa J. Breathless, he wrote a series of romantic adventures for teenage girl pulp magazines. In less than a year he had *Plummeted* out of romance also, into a full time job as a Wall Street stock analyst. Failing at that, in despair he thrust a Police Special .38 into his mouth and fired. He missed, only to die decades later of an undisclosed illness.

DEATH DATE FOR DORA
by McTack John Hardee

Installment 17: Reasons to Cry

I asked the bartender for Dora. He nodded in the direction of a blowsy, buxom babe sitting alone in the far corner booth, sullenly sipping a tall Glenlivet and Gatorade, obviously wishing for the old days. Her back was to the door, and the way she was sitting, you knew she'd turned her back on the world, too. This dame was dead to the universe that you and I spend our time in. She looked like a fighter who's down on one knee and almost out, and knows that the bell is still two minutes and ten seconds away. And yet there was still a trace of pizzazz about her, lurking somewhere under that stack of previously enticing flesh. It was hard to believe that this really was Dora Darling, the legendary "Gosh Girl" whose very name could still drive men crazy with remembered desire.

I slid onto a barstool across from her booth. She didn't look up. She wasn't seeing me or anything else in the room. Her mind was still on the night fame could have come home to stay – but didn't. The case dated way back to my rookie days on the force. I couldn't help smiling as I remembered it. It was one of those avant-garde "happenings" out on Long Island, just after the Korean War. The '50s were heady times for experimental artists of all kinds, and dancers were no exception. In those days Dora was running around with a radical choreographer named Rogelio, supposedly a pansy from a well-connected Cuban family. They were a real item. They say he was in love with her, the only time he ever had a thing for a woman. There was even talk of marriage. He believed in the woman as much as in her talent.

So Rogelio organized a special revue for her to star in. Used all his money. A pile of his family's, too. Hired a huge hall, gigantic orchestra, the works. A lighting guy from Hollywood. Uniformed usherettes from Paris. A lobby full of watercolors by sensitive guys. Smelly cheeses. The big production number was Dora's dance, based on the paintings of M.C. Escher. The daring climax of the piece was the "Möbius Strip Tease," which was designed to create the illusion of Dora's G-String coming on at the very moment she was taking it off.

The illusion failed – by ever so little – at each performance, and by the end of the week the theatre was raided by the cops. Everyone in the production was cited for indecent exposure and crimes against taste. Rogelio's father was a big political contributor, so he managed to keep the family name out of the papers. But young Rogelio's dream was shattered, and along with it, Dora's one shot at big time stardom. Like many "artistes," Rogelio's sanity had a glass jaw. Shortly after the collapse of the revue, they found him wandering naked through the Bronx Zoo, reciting Emily Dickenson poems to any animals that would listen. He was wearing lots and lots of eye liner, and claimed to be visiting from the future. They took him straight to Bellevue.

The diagnosis: acute eucalypsis. He was rushed to an arboretum with a fine eucalyptis grove, but it was already too late. Irreversible Koalian Regression had set in, and the poor guy withdrew. He spent his remaining few years in and around trees, unwashed, mumbling, an Easter – eggshell of a man, cracked beyond repair.

The last time Dora ever saw him alive, Rogelio was quietly chewing leaves on a private estate in Westchester County, the home of family friends. He was dressed in simple skins. She could not identify the leaves. Rogelio, or whatever it was that he had become, didn't seem to know her. She was finally persuaded to leave, her heart heavy, knowing that she could never forget the laughing Rogelio that once was – the young Cuban aristocrat with the flashing eyes and the 21st-Century notions. Even now, decades later, you could see that what remained of the "Gosh Girl" was still nursing one big fat hurt.

She stared vacantly into the past, drumming her empty ring finger on the formica table of the booth, an endless one-finger exercise that spelled "No Concertos for Dora." It was almost cruel to interrupt her reverie, but there was a murder to be solved, and Dora Darling just might have some answers. Our only remaining clue pointed to her. And the way I saw it, the good guys had only two chances left: very slim and anorexic; take your pick. Anyhow, I had to try.

I swallowed the last of my Boodles and Dr. Pepper and slid off the stool.

CASE HISTORY:
Failure At Plagiarism

It is quite amazing how many would-be authors are willing to steal not just stylistic traits and ideas from successful authors, but actually lift entire scenes, dialogue, even entire chapters. This author, boldly aping F. Scott Fitzgerald's masterpiece *The Great Gatsby*, didn't even attempt to mask the title – and was even arrogant enough to adopt the *nom de plume F. Scat FitzHerald!* Luckily for him, the publisher had never heard of either *Gatsby* or Scott Fitzgerald, since he spoke little English, most of his output being textbooks in Finnish and Basque. The name of the publishing house also might raise suspicions of plagiarism (or at least cheap imitation) among the suspicious: *HarporCullens Simen & Knopfster.*

The blatant plagiarism was noticed at the author's very first (which was also his very last) book signing at a major Manhattan bookseller, where he was severely beaten by a pack of pipe-smoking members of the *F. Scott Fitzgerald Memorial Brigade.* They were wearing cardigans, sported fedoras and had clearly been drinking.

The GREAT GADFLY
by F. Scat FitzHerald

Whenever I am tempted to think, or to opine, or even to consider anything about anybody, I remember what my father once said to me.

"Remember," he said, in that reservedly communicative way of his, "whenever you are tempted to think or to opine or even to consider anything about anybody else, remember that they haven't had the same advantages you've had, you rich little snot."

This advice was much in my mind upon my return last autumn from the East and the War and Yale, so I therefore immediately resolved to go back East. Since I should need some sort of career, I discussed prospects with my family, who have been prominent, well-to-do people in this Middle Western city for at least four hundred generations. My father agreed to support me for a decade or two while I learned the bond business, or even the bondage business. His exact parting words to me were "Ye-e-e-e-es, I suppose you ought to leave this Middle Western city – at least until we find a name for it – and begin a career back East, you pitiful, shallow, meaningless little slug."

After a brief delay (due to my accidentally traveling West for some weeks) I found myself back East once again, and dived into office routine. At first, because of its proximity to my work, I considered taking rooms on Central Park South, but the neighborhood was far too rough. When a fellow at the office suggested renting a house together on Long Island I agreed, despite the long commute. After all, I was young, I liked trees, and although the colleague ultimately was unable to share the place with me (he was hanged for murdering a Belgian town) I took it for myself.

The adjacent communities of North Bacon and South Bacon got their names because they are "strips" of land jutting out into Long Island Sound. Some city planners show flashes of true wit. Despite their proximity, there are major differences between the two towns. North Bacon is the place of sprawling estates, platoons of servants and sleek limousines. But my own tiny 17-room cottage was in modest South Bacon, where the underclass – struggling young bankers like myself – lived in comparative misery, limping along on a few thousand dollars an hour. Luckily my rent was a reasonable $2.75 a month in those days, so with careful scrimping and saving I was able to make ends meet.

Work was going well. Life, as far as life goes, was good. But in point of fact, I was lonely. Just about the time I was realizing this, a stroke of good fortune came my way, in the form of some old friends – relatives, really – who lived close by in one of the tonier neighborhoods of North Bacon.

My distant cousin Dipsy and her husband Todd rang me with an invitation to drinks and dinner on Saturday. And so, in the early sunset of a lovely summer day, I crossed the border into that wealthier world where my cousins lived. Even the wind smelled richer here. Bird songs seemed somehow more meaningful. Did the tall trees along these pampered roadways sense the opulence?

These were my thoughts as I motored toward Todd and Dipsy's rambling house up a long, long private drive bordered in rows of mustachia and purple euthanasia. A canopy of giant man-eating willows arched above my new

1922 Prattmobile Roadster, reflecting merrily in my windshield and on the shiny hood. In less than half an hour I drew up on the crunchy gravel before the marble columned portico of the mansion, which sat atop a high hillock overlooking the water. Stone walls surrounded the huge estate, as if begging an invitation to cocktails.

Todd was on the steps waiting to greet me, a bemused half-smile on his rugged, sunblown face. He was a huge, cruelly-muscled brute of fifteen, but with the body and mind of a much older man – say about seventeen. His rude peasant health belied the fact that he was one of Wall Street's most successful young brokers. One might easily have taken him for a prize fighter. Yet he was a brilliant and ruthless businessman, whom some considered the equal of a Bernie Madoff.

"Hello, Pick." He bounded from the porch and pumped my hand in his iron paw.

"Hello yourself, Todd," I riposted wittily, never at a loss for a bon mot, careful not to scream at the agonizing pressure of his bone-crushing grip.

As we entered the richly-appointed living room I was immediately aware of a couch. Upon it were two women in white. One was my cousin Dipsy. The other was not. Whoever she was, she was slender, small-breasted and allongée. For a moment it occurred to me that she might be dead. I was soon relieved to see, however, that she was moving very slightly, tilting her head back, as if to balance a tall stack of gold pieces on her forehead. She paid me no attention.

But Dipsy rushed toward me, extending her hands and smiling broadly.

"I'm w-w-wetting myself with happiness."

We embraced. Finally I was introduced to the tilting, lounging Miss Barker, who peered appraisingly into my eyes, as if she were selecting a polo mallet. The evening was becoming more interesting each moment.

We had thirty or forty cocktails as the gramophone sprayed jazz music into the summer wind. The drapes danced in the breeze, now alone, now together. Todd and

Dipsy avoided looking at each other, but looked frequently and intently at me. After I had wiped the dangling mucus from my nose, we had another cocktail.

"Todd has been reading deep books," Dipsy said. "Important books."

"Just books that make a lot of sense, darling," replied Todd in a strained voice.

Miss Barker tilted her head back as if it were about to explode and she didn't want to be near it when that happened. Her dress was whiter than ever in the sunset.

"This author sure knows what he's talking about when he says we should kill off everyone who's not like us. Makes a lot of sense," Todd repeated, pouring himself another cocktail.

"Your neighbor Gadfly is rich. Very rich," offered Miss Barker, then leaned back, framed in her fluttering white dress.

Dipsy was about to say something when a small cortège of colored maids and cook's helpers entered the room to announce dinner.

"Dinner," they said, with amusing directness. They can be such cute people sometimes. We all had another quick cocktail, then filed into the dining room. Conversation turned to neutral topics, such as Gadfly's amazing wealth and the simply marvelous parties he threw all season long.

"He sure is rich," said Miss Barker, throwing back her head and laughing in that tempting way of hers.

Just as we were finishing the Fish Fingers à la Meunière, washed down with another half dozen crisp dry martinis, the telephone jangled softly in the parlor. After a moment several butlers and an elderly negro retainer appeared and gathered around Todd's chair, whispering to him and pointing at the telephone. I sensed that the call was for Todd. He dabbed at his mouth with a strip of late 14th-Century silk Ming tapestry and rose from the table with a slight frown. He went inside and spoke softly and urgently into the phone.

After a moment, Dipsy slammed down her late 8th-Century Tang embroidered vealskin doily and followed him inside.

I turned to Miss Barker to discuss the socio-economic reality of 16th-Century Peru.

"Shut up, you hopeless, creepy little turd," she intoned in that thrilling low voice of hers. "I want to hear what's going on in there, where the real action is."

I cheerfully acquiesced, delighted that she was warming up to me.

Later, Todd and Miss Barker were in the living room, mixing some drinks. Dipsy took me by the hand and led me out onto the veranda, overlooking the water, the stables, the tennis courts, the airdrome, the race track and their private shopping center. We sat side by side on an 11th-Century Mayan wicker chaise longue. She spoke softly, but intently, in that delicious deep voice of hers.

"We don't know each other very well, though we're fourth cousins two-and-a-half times removed. Or is it second cousins four-and-a-half times removed? Anyway, you didn't come to my wedding. Or my high school graduation in Finland. Or even that time when I had those awful cramps."

“I wasn’t back from the war.”

“Yes, it was quite a long war,” she allowed. “Well, I’ve had a pretty bad time of it, Dick – that is your name, isn’t it? Rick? Zick? Anyway, I’ve become cynical. Especially since the baby was born.”

She leaned closer. Dipsy said softly, “You know where babies come from, don’t you, Mick?” After a brief pause she continued, pointing to the underside of her white dress. “From down under there,” she whispered, eyes wide with horror. “Oh, Flick, can you just imagine how disgusting!”

“Babies come from beneath white dresses?” I inquired, perplexed as a colored man at a country club tea.

“No, no, silly Brick – from even farther under than that! Babies actually come out of their mother’s – you know. At least mine did.”

I didn’t know, but was too sophisticated to let on, so I deftly changed the subject.

"I hear Todd's got chippies and floozies all over the place," I chirped merrily. "Wasn't that one of them phoning him a moment ago?"

At last it was night; a perfect windblown summery night. Somehow I had driven safely home. Removing my smoking jacket and stripping off my tie, I waved away the smoke. Suddenly eager for fresh air to clear my head of the evening's thrills, I stepped out into my back yard and ambled thoughtfully through the fragrant darkness, across the lawn that bordered Gadfly's enormous estate.

Suddenly I was aware of The Great Gadfly himself, prowling alone on the shore where his extensive lands met the water. At first I thought to greet him but decided to respect his privacy. After all, even rich men are men, and every man has his rights – at least if he's our kind of man. I watched Gadfly as cagily as a debutante eyeing her first Manhattan. Even in the pitch black he was the picture of perfect, unquestioned wealth. Yet he was in some ways mysterious. His hand kept darting in and out, in and out, in and out of his trouser front. What, I wondered aloud to myself in the night, could he be seeking there?

CASE HISTORY: Worst Sellers

Occasionally an author not only fails to write a best-seller, but creates a work so unimaginably dreadful that, although a publisher (for whatever reason) has agreed to release it, it sells virtually not at all.

The writer of these lines knows that feeling all too well. And he is not alone.

We know of one case in which, not only was the book a "worst seller," but was so egregiously dreadful that no copies are known to have reached even one single reader (even the author was refused his pre-release copies, lest he give some away to unsuspecting friends).

Further, this volume caused many already-bought new books to be returned to stores across the country.

The work in question, *A Policy of Lust*, by Jane Fortnum Snee, was a 4,105-page fictionalized novel about a 24-hour period in the life of Mrs. Mabel Criss (1881–1978), wife of the founder of *Mutual of Omaha.* It covers the day in 1928 when she was elected 2nd Vice President of the company – an epoch-making occasion that made her *Mutual*'s very first female officer!

This unique single-chapter work was an inner monologue, alternating philosophical speculation on the nature of insurance with incandescent sexual fantasies involving barnyard animals, scanty oilcloth garments and the backfield of the *University of Nebraska* football team.

Nobody bought it, because nobody ever had a chance to buy it. During production, the printer – a man of conscience and taste – ripped it out of the presses before the full run of 250 copies, destroying all but a dozen. Those were quickly condemned by both critics and legal authorities, and welded into an underground lead vault as "deleterious to public health and morals." Book shops everywhere were warned that some demented or taste-impaired customers, having heard rumors of the book's existence, might ask for it. In such cases, sales people were to inform the customer that the book had been "reverse-ordered," then confiscate an already purchased book from the customer, thereby creating the world's first known *negative book sales.*

Despite the resistance of many customers to this procedure, at last report, *A Policy of Lust* had amassed a total "inverse sale" of (-179) copies. This is a shining moment in *Catastrophic Comprehensive Failure* in the *Literature* category!

Writing And Pitching Screenplays

In recent decades, *Screenwriting* has evolved into the most glamorous writing category. Men and women who grind out scripts for movies or TV shows get lots of attention, make spectacular earnings and thus get to hang out with glamorous celebrities. They get to ride in long cars, even if they are short, and have brief marriages with women with huge breast implants or men with unexplainably bloated offshore bank accounts. When people who are otherwise uninterested in writing hear of these benefits, they instantly yearn to be screenwriters.

Everyone has seen hundreds of movies. So how hard could it be to write just one? Judging from the quality of the "blockbusters" and "heartwarming romantic comedies" showing in multiplex cinemas and crowding the shelves at video stores, it would seem to be pretty easy for anyone to write for the screen.

We have all heard some friend say, "Hey, I've got a great idea for a movie!" and then enthusiastically describe what is invariably either (a) *Not* a great – or even good – idea for a movie; or (b) A great idea for a movie that has already been made many times – it's just that the enthusiastic would-be screenwriter doesn't know it. That's all right. He'll find out soon enough, when he is laughed out of his first meeting by professionals who *do* know that his great idea has been produced dozens of times.

But let's say that you learn the right format. You work on "structure" and get the "dramatic curve" right. Your computer's screenplay program assembles your work neatly across the obligatory 125 pages, leaving "lots of air." Snappy, short dialogue. No camera instructions – "directors just hate that." *They* want to be the ones to decide what the audience should be looking at.

Now all you need to to guarantee success is to have the right "concept," so whoever ends up buying it can be thanked, on Oscar night, for having "vision." So, Aspiring Screenwriter, what's your "vision" (also called "concept")?

CASE HISTORY:
Vision/Concepts Guaranteed To Get Your Movie Rejected

We all learn from the classics. Following are thumbnail concepts that would certainly have destroyed any chance of these great films becoming the masterpieces they are. Learn from them!

The Dirty Dozen

- *A singing horse entertains at a gala soirée in a Nazi stronghold.*
- *Allied trolls, hiding inside the horse, jump out and blow up the Nazis.*
- *Julie Andrews, not Lee Marvin, trains the commando raiders.*

The Sound Of Music

- *The hills are alive with the sound of gunfire as a tank duel erupts.*
- *The Trapp Family is captured and executed by a band of tone-deaf French music-haters.*
- *A sudden tornado leaves a little dog named Toto marooned in the Alps.*

Casablanca

- *Seven dwarfs beg Rick to get them letters of transit, or at least letters of credit.*
- *Instead of "As Time Goes By," Sam plays "My Baby Does the Hanky-Panky."*

- *Louis, the Vichy French officer, strangles Rick with a telephone cord, then becomes a Perrier French officer.*

Mary Poppins

- *Mary carries a rain slicker instead of an umbrella.*
- *The chimney sweep molests her. She turns him over to the bobbies.*
- *Family develops cholera. Mary's songs can't help; kids are medevac'd to Berne for treatment.*

Citizen Kane

- *Film opens with the dying Charles Foster Kane crying out "Hey, where's my sled?"*
- *Mr. Bernstein converts Kane's luxury hideaway Xanadu into a reform synagogue.*
- *Entire production is done in blackface.*

Gone With The Wind

- *The South wins on a technicality.*
- *Rhett is simply mad for Ashley, who spurns his advances and beats him up.*
- *Scarlett slaves day and night to become a travel agent in New Jersey. "As God is my witness, I'll never fly Tourist again."*

Taxi Driver

- *Pat Boone plays the weapons-crazy Vietnam vet, Travis Bickle.*
- *Cheerful musical with Billy Crystal, Robin Williams is set in sunny Hawaii.*
- *The line, "You talkin' to me?" is replaced by "Ontogeny recapitulates phylogeny!"*

Jaws

- *First titled "Beaks," homage to "The Birds." Giant White Robins terrorize a back yard.*
- *Later titled "Pincers," homage to "Them." A Giant White Ant terrorizes a company picnic.*
- *Opens with New Englanders barbecuing a Great White Shark on the beach.*

Beverly Hills Cop

- *A singing horse entertains everyone at the police station.*
- *Terrence Stamp and seven dwarfs capture Eddie Murphy.*
- *Julie Andrews leads Beverly Hills children over the hill to a lovely valley.*

Rocky

- *Down-and-out club chess player wins World Championship.*
- *Down-and-out dog trainer wins American Kennel Club beagle championship.*
- *Down-and-out actor writes blockbuster hit movie about down-and-out writer.*

E.T. – The Extraterrestrial

- *E.T. has a singing horse that entertains the earthlings.*
- *The children, fearing pedophile aliens, strangle E.T. with a telephone cord.*
- *E.T. becomes a U.S. citizen; marries Britney Spears; opens a 7-11 store.*

The Exorcist

- *The possessed girl strikes a deal with Satan, who makes her the first woman president.*
- *The Linda Blair role is played by Julie Andrews.*
- *Father Damian's singing horse stomps the devil to death.*

The Godfather

- *Don Vito Corleone finds the olive oil business more lucrative than crime – and lots less violent.*
- *Kay Corleone is possessed by the devil and joins the Tattaglia Brothers' family.*
- *Sonny is saved from the ambush by a little dog named Toto.*

Rambo

- *John Rambo, Ph.D. proves that economic sanctions are more effective than violence.*
- *Rambo goes undercover as a song-and-dance man in Ho Chi Minh City.*
- *Rambo becomes a down-and-out club fighter in Philadelphia.*

Animal House

- *Aliens join the fraternity, causing much hilarious hi-jinx with outer space beer.*
- *An anthrax epidemic claims the lives of everyone in the frat house.*
- *The frat adopts a cute little dog from Kansas.*

Silence Of The Lambs

- *Crazy, savage Dr. Lecter is played not by Anthony Hopkins but Danny de Vito.*
- *The psychotic murderer's "signature" is not a moth in victims' throats, but a badger.*
- *Cannibalistic shrink responds to therapy; is cured; marries a woman senator from Maine.*

Saturday Night Fever

- *Tony, dissatisfied with life in the City Center Ballet, becomes an international jewel thief.*
- *Mikhail Baryshnikov and Beyoncé challenge Tony to a break dancing contest.*
- *Aliens mistake revolving disco lights for an enemy UFO; attack Brooklyn.*

On The Waterfront

- *Terry, a contender for the middleweight crown, kills a waterfront priest who looks just like a young Karl Malden.*
- *Stephen Sondheim sets words to the Bernstein score; cheerful longshoremen sing and dance.*
- *The nice girl, America's first lady dock worker, strips on weekends to earn union dues.*

The Magnificent Seven

- *Sleepy, Dopey and Bashful defect from The Magnificent Ten, leaving only seven.*
- *All seven have singing horses who perform a Bach chorale for the besieged town.*
- *Yul Brynner's role is played by Nathan Lane.*

Close Encounters Of The Third Kind

- *The French UFOlogist is really an alien UFOlogist in disguise.*
- *Roy's brusque Duddy-Kravitz-like behavior offends the kewpie dolls from outer space; they microwave him.*
- *Movie is titled "Planet of the ARP Synthesizers."*

CASE HISTORY: Catastrophically Failed Screenplays

Following are two examples of scripts that *Plummeted* because of the principles *Too Much Something* (genre flavor) and *Too Little Something* (probably writing talent). That said, the screenwriters have not only allowed us to include their names, they have insisted strenuously on it. This is good, because it shows their willingness to move ahead to *Catastrophic Comprehensive Failure* (see Chapter One for definitions).

Genre:
Unremitting Ethnic Urban Inner-City Streetwise Violence

B-A-A-A-A-D MOTHA'S HIT DA 'HOOD

By Clarence "Big Ice" Jackson & Leroy "15-X" Shabazz

OPEN ON BLACK FREEZE FRAME.

MUSIC UP: "We Be Ba-a-a-a-a-a-d" by Pigballs & Da Mothafucka's (OS).

PIGBALLS (OS)

We come from Compton an we be
ba-a-a-a-ad,
And we knowin dat our bitches
ain't fuckin no cops,
We runnin wif da gangstas and
all a dat sheee-it,
Mah heat's always ready and mah
juice is on da street cause ya
know dat dey ain't no way at we
put up wif all dat shee-it,
mah man, cuz …

CHORUS OF MOTHAFUCKA'S (OS)

Wat it is? Wat it is? Wat it is?
Wat da fuck it is?

PIGBALLS (OS)
It be dat we be ba-a-a-a-a-a-ad,
Ah say ba-a-a-a-a-a-a-a-ad,
Ah means ba-a-a-a-a-a-d,
Wat da fuckWat da fuckWat da
fuck Wat da fuck
Our bitches be ba-a-a-a-ad,
our gangstas be ba-a-a-a-ad,
an We be ba-a-a-a-a-d!

CHORUS OF MOTHAFUCKAS (OS)
Wat it is? Wat it is? Wat it is?
Hey hey hey wat da fuck it is?

PIGBALLS (OS)
It be dat we be ba-a-a-a-a-ad!

(Music fades out on unadorned fuckin drum rhythm.)

FADE UP REAL FAST TO:

1. INT. NIGHT. BIG RASTUS'S POOL HALL in South Central fuckin L.A. ERNIE DA CLIPPER, 22, street smart, tough, with scars in places where you ain't even got no fuckin places, holds his

.44 magnum right in the fuckin sweaty face of JAMES DA DOPE DEALER, 22, and fuckin scared fuckin shitless. Mothafucka owes Ernie big time an the cocksucka go'ne pay, big time, no sheee-it. BIG RASTUS, 23, and DA BOYZ (ALL 20) stand around, they watchin wif interes.

2. INT. NIGHT. POOL HALL. FEATURE ERNIE AND JAMES.

JAMES

Hey, fuck, man, go fuckin easy wid dat thing, fucker go off, you doan jes cooooooool it, mothafucka.

ERNIE

Who you callin mothafucka, mothafucka? Dis fuckin thing go off, you fuckin head fuckin goin off da same fuckin time, cocksucka mothafucka.

JAMES

(pretty fuckin agitated)

Whooooo dere, take it easy, mah man,
din mean nothin.
Ooooo-eee! Jes stay cool now, mah man.

ERNIE

Where dat fuckin money you fuckin owe me?

JAMES

Ah'll git it, ah swear ah will!

Ah jes needs a lil mo time.

ERNIE
Already give you all the fuckin time you fuckin need.

3. INT. NIGHT. POOL HALL. Ernie pistol-whips James somethin fierce. Blood splatterin everywhere. James scream. Ernie shoots James in the lef elbow. James he scream again.

ERNIE
Wuzzat? Cain't fuckin take it, huh?

JAMES
(gaspin real fuckin loud)
Ah gits ya da fuckin money, jes need 10 fuckin seconds.
Ah gots it in mah shoe raht cheer.

James takes off his shoe, and sure nuff, they lots of money in it. Ernie smiles real fuckin sinister.

ERNIE
Dat's all ah wanted to fuckin know, mothafucka.

4. SLO-MO SEQUENCE. Ernie shoots James all over the fuckin place, then takes an axe and chops him into little bloody fuckin pieces while Big

Rastus & Da Boyz laugh and laugh they fuckin heads off. Ernie leans down, takes the money from James blood filled shoe, fans the thick wad of fuckin bills, and smiles real fuckin contented.

ERNIE
(to Rastus & Da Boyz)
So, where ya wanna fuckin eat?

FADE TO FUCKIN BLACK REAL SLOW

Genre:
Unremittingly Sappy Social Commentary Romance

CHICK FLICK

By Cyndie Sharpe & Syd Morty

FADE IN:

1. EXT. BEACH, DAY. MUSIC: Pachelbel's "Canon" plays as CORRIE, 22 and single and darkly beautiful, walks hand in hand along Malibu Colony beach with a Viking-featured HUNK. This is REX, 23 and nauseatingly handsome; sunblown, windcragged, in fashionably faded knee-rent jeans. He wears no shirt. His abs ripple as he walks and his buns throb through the denim. Corrie, former Atalissa, Iowa beauty queen, is a Ph.D. anthropologist; Rex is a self-made

zillionaire polo-playing stock broker. They've been an item since grad school at Cal State Trancas, but all that is about to change.

2. EXT. BEACH, DAY. ANGLE ON REX.
Rex broods, splashing through ankle-deep surf. Corrie senses something amiss.

CORRIE
Hey, babe, what is it?

Rex remains silent, gazes out to sea as they walk.

CORRIE
(continuing after a perplexed pause)
You're quiet today, honey-poo … too quiet.

REX
(sighing)
Corrie, we've got to talk. Things can't go on this way.

CORRIE
"This way?" What way? Isn't everything just perfect? Aren't we simply the most scrumptious couple simply EVER?

3. CLOSE ON REX. He stops abruptly, turns and faces Corrie. He releases her hand.

REX

There's something you have to know.
I've been seeing someone else.
It started out so innocently -
friendship at the health club.
Then it developed into something
that's bigger than both of us.
Bigger than all of us.
I'm sorry, Corrie, but I've got to
follow my heart …

3. TIGHT on CORRIE's pale, shocked face as she reacts to this tidbit.

REX

(continuing OS)

… and my heart has led me to Bob.

4. FAST PUSH IN. Corrie's face fills frame.

CORRIE

(gasping)

To … Bob?

5. FEATURE REX, smiling in ecstasy as he rehearses Bob's delights.

REX

Yes, Bob - he's just so dreamy! Smart and funny - not at all like you. And much taller. A real smooth dancer, too. So I'm leaving you, Corrie. Today I move in with Bob!

CUT BACK TO:

6. FULL FRAME of Corrie's dead, shocked face. She is so motionless we might even consider a FREEZE FRAME.

CORRIE
(stunned)
Bob?

REX
(OS)
It's over, Corrie. O-v-e-r.

CORRIE
(to herself)
He's leaving me for … a man!

The letters o-v-e-r ECHO louder and louder, drowning out Pachelbel. Lorrie remains motionless. A single salty tear dribbles down her cheek.

7. FOLLOW the TEAR, PUSH IN for ECU of tear, which then MORPHS into a PUDDLE in the gutter outside the NATURAL FOODSTUFF EMPORIUM.

8. EXT. DAY, EMPORIUM MONTAGE. MUSIC UP LOUD: "Born to be Wild." Corrie emerges from the store with two bags of groceries, each with a baguette sticking out of the end. She approaches her car at the curb. A convoy of BRADLEY FIGHTING VEHICLES whooshes past, each splashing her as it moves through the puddle. A DOBERMAN bitch bites her on one leg while a male FOX TERRIER lifts his leg and pees on the other. She drops the groceries in the puddle. One BFV sideswipes and wrecks her car, which explodes in flames. A passing WORKMAN knocks her down with his ladder. She falls in the puddle among her mooshy groceries. WATER CRESS tangles in her hair. A FISH dropped by a SEAGULL lands down her cleavage, wriggling its way ever deeper down her shirt. FIREMEN responding to the blazing car hose her down, repeatedly knocking her to the ground. Her clothes shred. SIX RASTAFARIAN GANGSTA RAPPERS drive past and shoot her with handguns, wounding her but not lethally. The workman returns and, oblivious, knocks her down again with his ladder. An AMBULANCE responding to the gunshots accidentally runs over her leg, then backs up and runs over her arm. INTERCUT shots of the baguettes crushed by the tires, the fish escaping deeper into the puddle, BLOOD mingling

with mayonnaise, etc. TWO PARAMEDICS try to lift Corrie onto a stretcher, but keep dropping her. At last they slide her into the back of the ambulance and drive away. The doors fly open and Corrie and the stretcher fall out and roll down the Pacific Coast Highway as the paramedics, oblivious, disappear over the horizon. The stretcher zooms over a cliff into the ocean as there is a BLINDING FLASH and HUGE EXPLOSION followed by an ATOMIC MUSHROOM CLOUD.

CUT TO:

9. INT. DAY. EMERGENCY ROOM.
SCOTT MARC GIMPEL, M.D., 24, bends over Corrie as she comes to. He is devastatingly handsome, masculine, sensitive - and still single! Corrie is a mess; in tatters, covered with cinders, strontium-90 particles, blood clots and one piece of stubborn baguette that clings to her nose.

10. CORRIE'S POV. She sees Scott's smiling face beaming down at her, but can only groan.

SCOTT
(smiling)

Well, little lady - looks like you've
had yourself one heck of a day!

FADE TO BLACK

Failure At Poetry

Writing poetry is arguably one of the most subjective of all artistic enterprises, and consequently the hardest to evaluate. It is often hard to tell whether a given poem is an example of *Futuristic Anarchic Deconstructionism* ... or random typing by a housebroken chimpanzee. Does it mean anything to the reader? Did it mean anything to the writer? The publisher? Has the poem actually been published, or was it written in pencil on a supermarket shopping bag? Were royalties paid? Did the check clear? Has the poet committed suicide yet?

All of these questions and more are germane to the critical process, and play a part in the quest for *Failure at Poetry*.

Once upon a time poems rhymed. They were composed within a certain rhythmic framework. To write a meaningful, moving, successful poem required a high degree of literary skill.

Fortunately, that is a thing of the past. Nowadays, the most important element in poetry is how it lines up on the page, and if its meaning – assuming the *Meaning* default setting is activated on the Poetry Writing Program – is obscured cleverly enough. If so, there is always the risk that the poem may actually succeed. Indeed it may become beloved enough to be included in textbooks or collections for poetry lovers.

Some poems walk a careful line between absurd and "modern." Following is an example of a work that has some rhyme, and has a visible form – most of the way. The intent of the poem is, however, unclear, which is where its charm resides for *Failure Aspirants* who may wish to use this as a model for their own inspiration.

CASE HISTORY:
Poem With Rhyme and Form, Sort Of

PILLARS OF DESPAIR
by
Kuen McRod

Alas, the vacuous emptiness;
Yon fronds dangle with phthisic savagery, and

Thought hangs as if by chance, and yet so heavy on the spleen.

Ah woe, such hardy tardiness;
Fond ponds wrangle with mystic imagery, and
Fraught fangs within a stance, regret so heavy on the spleen.

Oy vey, the Mardi Gras's a mess;
Wan bonds mangled by plastic surgery, and
Naught sang within the dance, so wet, so heavy on the spleen.

Alas, ah woe, ay ay and arrrgghhh,
I feel so doggone down;
If only Big Naomi had invited me to dinner last Wednesday night and cooked that pork roast I like so much with all those potatoes and oven-browned sauerkraut and applesauce and all the trimmings, maybe a couple of glasses of beer,
I wouldn't wanna leave this town.

Oh, yeahhhhhhh.

The post-WWII years have increased worldwide awareness of Latin American culture, particularly in the visual arts (vivid shawls; cute pots; brightly colored murals depicting thick peasants, corn, machetes!); music (hip-swiveling rhythms, whacking of odd-shaped percussion instruments); kaleidoscopic political changes; and of course a literature to encompass it all.

Being the dominant language of the Western Hemisphere south of the Rio Grande, Spanish is emerging slowly upon the consciousness of English-speakers as a vehicle for artistic expression. Many *Failure Aspirants* have begun to express themselves in Spanish as a second language. Luckily most of those attempts have been third or fourth rate, occasionallly skyrocketing to second rate. Following is a model of a Third-and-a-Half Rate work by a solidly third rate "modernista," whose misuse of the lovely Spanish language is surpassed only by the lack of clarity in the poem's content. This work has surely edged the poet close to *Plummet.*

ORACIÓN SIN LITANÍA
by
Darén Rubío *

Y ¿cuál será el otoño que me mata?
¿Qué martillo vendrá del Corazón aquel día,
Con seda celeste?

Me habló el chapulín de voz baja.
Me platicó de cosas extrañas.
Valles. Fuego. Y torturas con el agujero de plata.

Llegó el cura en el Buick.
Sus uñas hablaban del Sacramento, y sus ojos
Brillaban de lodo.

Hay tantas montañas y tan poco tiempo.

* [NOTE: The poet's name has been changed, by the appropriate consulate, to protect his country's reputation by masking the author's nationality.]

[TRANSLATION: *Prayer Without Litany* by Darén Rubío]

And which will be the autumn that kills me?
What hammer will come from the Heart that day,
With heavenly silk?

The grasshopper spoke to me in a quiet voice.
He chatted to me about strange things.
Valleys. Fire. And torture with the silver needle.

The priest arrived in the Buick.
His fingernails spoke of the Sacrament, and his eyes
Gleamed with mud.

There are so many mountains and so little time.]

When all else fails, *Failure at Poetry* can usually be induced by writing in an unfamiliar (or preferably a nonexistent!) language!

CASE HISTORY:
Literature Failure Through Incomprehensibility

[In his exasperatingly endless career, the fabled international literary mastermind Ezra Kilo (1878?-2009?) exhausted the possibilities of the Earth's most widely-read literary languages. In order to pursue his poetic inspiration to its fullest extent, he felt obliged to create an entirely new language, one he considered rich and subtle enough to bear the full weight of his genius. Unburdened by false modesty, he named this literary vehicle Ezra Kilo Language (EKL). *He wrote neither a grammar nor a dictionary of EKL, consistently refusing to explain any of its elements. Whenever asked for details, he smirked and placed his finger cryptically across his lips.*

Since Dr. Kilo was the only person who understood the language, his poetic output over the last 15 years of his life was restricted to an audience of one – himself, although his wife Gedda often humored him by pretending to intuit the meaning his verses. She was such an enabler.

Despite the foregoing disadvantages, against all odds, some of Ezra Kilo's work has found its way into the canon, fertile material for imaginative scholars' interpretation. Perhaps his best loved poem, maybe because it is also his briefest, is the tauntingly incomprehensible Thuffwyl Tryfinick, *presumably a commentary on an indecipherable quote from some unknown other person, the previously unheard-of "Hirkla Vlupiw." Could this be another level of meaning – or more likely, the poet's joke within a prank within a chortle? We may never be sure. But we are confident that, in the fullness of time, the name Ezra Kilo will have* Plummeted *to the dungeons of* Catastrophic Comprehensive Failure *in the* Poetry *category! This would surely have brought joy to the gruff old scholar. – The Editors]*

THUFFWYL TRYFINICK
by
Ezra Kilo

"Tarl flisfeg oll minnaqal, sta!"
Hirkla Vlupiw (1567?-1639?)

Thredl ve wharmal veduul pa,
Gezorna traf ti kalooma.
Geel. Whegga tol, fillia tol
dunni wo ladarra swip lakooma.

Hardl ge faloorn veduul pa,
Tarsturra kik lal ti pasoolka.

Heeka wol, zilecki pol
dunni wo tarolla swip amoolka.

Tirrup tirrup ska, fillo hon bezorn!

[*NOTE: No widely accepted translation of these lines has been produced to date. However, forensic linguists from the* J.R.R. Tolkien Society*;* Georgtown University's Institute of Languages and Linguistics *and other prominent cultural philological organizations have advanced the theory that Thuffwyl Tryfinick may mean "Shopping List." This suggests that Dr. Kilo may have been even more eccentric and obstructionist than his biographies suggest. – The Editors]*

CHAPTER SIX

FAILING AT EMPLOYMENT AND CAREERS

by Scofield J.M.H. "Scooter" Bradford, IV

"Scooter" earned his way into the Super Failers' Hall of Fame *by successfully* Failing *at a wide range of careers, including (but not limited to) coaching women's volleyball; urban planning; talent management (a mute ventriloquist who had earlier failed as a mime; a deaf Hungarian soprano; a talking salmon) and nearly a*

decade in the U.S. Foreign Service. There he disgraced himself in a series of minor consular duties in far-flung "hardship posts." "Scooter" consistently tried and failed to help stranded Americans recover luggage; pay parking fines; or simply get out of the country, in destinations as unwelcoming as Ushuaia, Tierra del Fuego (Argentina); Edinburgh of the Seven Seas, Tristan da Cunha (the most remote archipelago on Planet Earth); and finally at Maseru, capital of the tiny landlocked African kingdom of Lesotho, where he achieved persona non grata *status "for every imaginable reason," as the local Chief of Police explained it.*

"I never met a Golden Opportunity I was unable to sidestep," he cheerfully observes. After successfully bankrupting Norm's Wholesale Spoon World *(Xenia, OH), "Scooter" turned down a succession of part time night watchman jobs from coast to coast. He finally took a position as Chief Day Watchman at the men's room in Union Station in Washington, D.C., but was fired partway through his first shift. "We thought he was watching the men just a little too closely," was all his supervisor would say. – The Editors*

What's So Great About Working, Anyway?

Work is widely considered an important part of a person's career. Accounts vary, but most observers seem to agree that a major attraction of work is its tendency to provide *a regular source of income.* Little else about work offers much appeal. Income is pretty much the whole story. Traditionalists consider income useful as a practical way of getting a steady supply of money. People tend to be fond of money because it can buy or do things we cannot make or do for ourselves. For these reasons, many individuals choose to work for money rather than simply stealing or borrowing it. However, almost nobody prefers working to inheritance as a means of acquiring money.

[For more on money and its drawbacks, see Chapter Three on Failing at Business And Finance. – *The Editors]*

Most employment involves working for others: individuals, small companies, governments or huge international conglomerates. The terms of employment generally require performance of certain duties, or delivering something of value to the employer, for which the employee gets money, usually in the form of a salary. There may also be company benefits, like health insurance, a payroll savings plan, profit sharing, use of a company car or other facilities, the opportunity for bonuses and other financial or social extras. These benefits (as well as pay raises) are generally tied to performance, usually to *good* performance.

People who hire other people know all about that.

Therefore, when trying to "succeed" at getting a job, the trick is for applicants to convince a prospective employer that (a) they are well qualified to perform the duties, or deliver the values, that the company requires; and (b) they will be a reliable, conscientious and agreeable addition to the company's work force – in other words, a good performer.

The challenge for those of us who pursue the *Joy of Failure*, is to avoid convincing prospective employers that we will be good performers who are worth hiring. There are always more people than jobs. This is a matter of concern for those who sincerely wish to find a job. For *Plummeters*, who have no unrealistic desire for success, it is good news.

Nuts And Bolts Of Job Failure

Landing a good job is very much a matter of attitude and technique. This means, by extension, that *not* landing a good job is *also* a matter of attitude and technique. It's a matter of deciding which attitude, and which technique, to employ. Once you master the loser's attitude and technique, *Failure* is all but certain. Hard work is necessary to accomplish any unquestionable, irreversible *Failure*. But it is occasionally possible to lose out on a job inquiry by going straight for the jugular with "quick kill" tactics like:

- Not applying for the job in the first place
- Never showing up for the interview – ha ha, the joke's on them!
- Sending a drunken stinky wildly flailing derelict to sub for you
- Showing up a day late, at the wrong company

However, if circumstances unavoidably require your presence in the right place at the right time, you can still make things wrong.

You Are Not Necessarily Beaten !

Simply turn to any or all of the following *Loser Techniques.* When conscientiously applied, they are virtually guaranteed to help you fail when applying for a job.

Advanced Losers, past masters of these techniques, have been known to be physically removed from interviews – even at companies owned or directed by close relatives! But those are the true legends. Beginners should not reasonably expect that degree of *Plummet,* although by steadfastly employing the techniques we recommend, they will be well on their way to disaster only minutes into the job interview. What are these techniques? Let's look at them one at a time.

Loser Techniques That Will Set You Free

(1) *Maintain a Really Bad Attitude.* Negativity rules! Just keep thinking that you don't deserve the job. (You have the advantage of this being true!) You're surely not qualified for it. And even if you were, because of your toxic personality, the company wouldn't want anyone like you working among them. By keeping those thoughts fixed constantly in your mind throughout the job hunting process, you can greatly enhance your chances for succeeding at *Failure.*

(2) Cultivate the Habit of Scowling. Hang your head glumly. Look as defeated as possible. Refuse to look anyone in the eye, especially the interviewer. Alternatively: stare at the interviewer's crotch (whether male or female), and murmur mysteriously to yourself, mouthing indistinct leering utterances. Sigh occasionally. By carefully rehearsing these simple bad attitude procedures, they will be second nature to you, available whenever you need them – even long after the

prospective employer has turned you down, or (if you're really proficient at radiating negativity) thrown you roughly out into the street. Indeed, with a little perseverance, bad attitude can become first nature to you!

(3) *Dress For Failure.* Naïve dolts, trotting blindly along like so many sheep on the pathway to "happiness," are advised to "Dress for Success." The very idea is bitterly laughable. The presumption is that if you look like a winner, you will be treated like a winner, and therefore automatically rocket to "success" not only in business, but also in your personal, social and community life. Please. Please. This shallow notion seems to work all too often for all too many fools. So our recommended antidote is, "Dress for Plummeting." Wear any damn thing you like, carefully avoiding any suggestion of stylishness, good taste or cleanliness. (See *Chapter Two: Failure at Love and Sex*, for useful hints on *Plummet* dressing.)

(4) *Include Blatant Lies in Your Resumé.* Nobody likes a liar. You knew that, right? So – put that knowledge to work for you! Sample untruths: You have a medical degree from Harvard, a law degree from Oxford and a Doctor of Divinity from Vatican State. You invented the telephone. You are an Armenian prince in exile. You swam the Pacific in three days when you were only 15.

One “red arrow” lie that always works is to *claim to be president of the company for which you are interviewing!* If possible, also incorporate sordid details about arrests for criminal activities, even if no such events occurred.

(5) *Invent Overly Impressive References.* This is an important sub-category of blatant lying, which we append here because most companies place great emphasis on the recommendations of previous employers. There are two highly effective tacks to take when perpetrating this *Big Lie.*

- List extremely famous personages in business and government, none of whom – of course – have ever heard of you. That way, in the highly unlikely event your application survives the interview phase and reaches the fact-checking phase, your lie will be all the more barefaced, assuming the Human Resources Department even succeeds in contacting your supposed supporter. Suggested references might include the current Chairman of Sony or Microsoft; some high-profile astronaut or other national hero; world renowned celebrities, rock stars, sports heroes or other glitterati.

- Using as references people who were dead long before you were even born adds punch to the fib!

So go for it. Stretch your imagination with "recommendations" from the likes of Gen. George Patton; Queen Marie of Romania; Babe Ruth; Henry Ford; Benedict Arnold; Saint Francis of Assisi.

CASE HISTORY:
The Outrageous Resumé Route

Below is an excellent example of the *"Liar Liar, Pants On Fire"* school of resumé writing. Our staff have verified that the man who wrote it, and distributed it *via* the ingenious technique of the *Chain Resumé,* not only never landed a job interview from it, but was relentlessly pursued and savagely beaten by several HR directors. According to our last reports, he had petitioned for political asylum in Paraguay, and was bussing tables in a small family owned restaurant in the suburbs of Asunción. In lieu of salary (he had no working papers) he was allowed to keep whatever was left on patrons' plates. We may only suppose that he is very happy.

Resumé

[Name withheld pending notification of relatives]
[Address withheld due to Privacy Act]
[Telephone no longer in service]

2004-present: Catch-as-catch-can freelance advertising and marketing work. Piano playing for tips in scruffy waterfront dives patronized chiefly by layabouts, drug fiends, prostitutes, used car salesmen in checkered sports jackets with Bovril stains on the sleeve, down-and-out former ad hacks, dwarfs, mountebanks, swindlers, con men, con women, con hermaphrodites, cutthroats, cutthumbs, cutlets, child pornographers, jaded children, the occasional honeymoon couple from Elkhart, IN (stumbling in briefly by mistake), and the woman they called "Big Naomi," with a set of gams and a rack of casabas to make a strong man moan aloud. But I digress.

2003-2004: Emperor of China, Asia. Responsible for unremittingly despotic rule over nearly one billion enslaved coolies. Re-routed the Yangtze and Yellow rivers. Invented both rice and tea. Ruled with iron fist, which never rusted despite many rainstorms. Brought enlightenment to dozens by creating paper and pencils. Generated great regional conflict (invasions, plagues, mass destruction of neighboring lands); choked off all international trade decades ahead of projections! Designed and built the Greater Wall of China, extending from northern Paraguay to the eastern border of Norway. Would have accomplished more had I not been treacherously assassinated by a trusted aide.

2000-2003: Three-time World Champion figure skater; singing sword swallower with Ringling Brothers circus (Moultrie, GA unit); U.S. National Spelling Bee Gold Medalist (Senior Division); foiled a dramatic armed kidnap attempt (Xenia, OH, 3/16/02); was granted U.S. patent #52,882,016 (Aerosol Penis Repellent); met Pele. Elected CEO and Chairman of Litton Industries. Founded and operated a chain of store front kindergartens in depressed inner city neighborhoods (Baltimore, MD; Paoli, PA; Grosse Pointe, MI; Shaker Heights, OH; Brentwood, CA). Learned to yodel.

1997-2000: Inmate #607554 (Trustee), Federal Penitentiary, Joliet, IL. (Falsely imprisoned – incompetent attorney unable to defend against charge that I murdered Belgium.) Released thirty-five years early for exemplary behavior. Established first drive-thru prison laundry; earned medical and legal degrees while still "inside"; researched and cured cancer; through my personally run education-rehabilitation program I converted all inmates into outstanding citizens, most with advanced degrees (mainly Doctor of Divinity).

1990-1997: President of France.

1982-1990: General Officer, U.S. Army. Commanded European and Asian troops; devised and implemented strategy that resulted in American conquest of the world. Invented the WAC. Dated a woman who looked like Debbie Reynolds. Was the first American to fly to the moon on gossamer wings. Briefly President of the New York Stock Exchange (May 4th 1983). Youngest American ever to die of old age. Wrote and directed blockbuster hit movie, "The Mormon Tabernacle Chainsaw Massacre." Invented and marketed 3-D for live theatre. Was very handsome in a craggy sort of way.

1975-1982: Head Janitor, Ed's Auto World, Ballinger, TX. Able to use two brooms simultaneously; invented astonishing new technique to dry clean cars; entrusted with many keys. First human to walk on the surface of the sun (10/12/79 at about 4:00 PM local time). Taught underwater breathing to Jewish War Veterans (Montpelier, VT). Earned simultaneous doctorates from Heidelberg, Yale and Buenos Aires universities and Albany State Teachers' College.

1965-1975: Reckless youthful behavior.

1960-1965: I forget.

1950-1960: Birth. Drooling, a dawning awareness of the universe. Mastered the Literary Canon; acquired fluency in 75 languages, some of which can be identified. Advised Harry S Truman and Gen. George Marshall on strategies for post-WWII Europe. Learned to whistle. Repainted Sistine Chapel ceiling in much brighter colors. Invented shrapnel, Lionel Trains, the paper bag.

References upon request.

---

(4) *Exhibit Violent Tendencies.* This ploy, which might be termed "losing through intimidation," can consist of any combination of these elements:

Stare maniacally at the interviewer, showing your teeth and licking your lips menacingly. If you can arrange for flecks of foam to appear in your mouth, you'll be that much ahead of the game. Growl if possible, and make sudden short feints in the direction of the interviewer's head. Occasionally say "heh heh heh," and rub your hands together. Look furtively about as if seeking a weapon. It may not always be possible to actually come armed with lethal weapons when you arrive for the meeting, but it is easy for the imaginative *Loser* to give the impression of "packing heat," or worse. A piece of fruit, a rolled-up magazine, a clump of mud (or other darkly stinky substance) bundled into your breast pocket, or a suspicious bulge anywhere but the front of the trousers will arouse fear of possible danger lurking there. Similarly, a vial of white powder placed with a smirk on the interviewer's desk will reveal that you are not averse to carrying (a) weaponized anthrax or (b) socialized cocaine.

(5) *Imply Fondness For, and Support of, Sexual Deviance.* During the interview, and also on your resumé, insert sly mention of close friends and family implicated in the disappearance of entire Boy Scout and Brownie troops. Speak proudly of your lifesized, anatomically correct, real-wool ewe with the renewable inner lining; of your prize collection of whips, teddies and pre-owned *Depends* ™; of your ambition to soar beyond the wildest imaginings of Krafft-Ebing and Sade.

(6) *Play the "Minority" Card.* This tactic can be approached productively from *any of three* standpoints.

- Pretend to be – despite any outward appearances – an existing minority. (Select whichever ethnos or non-mainstream lifestyle you think will make the interviewer most uncomfortable.)

- Reveal in loud, crude terms how much you hate minorities, and how you refuse on religious grounds to work alongside anyone from other groups. This is especially effective when the interviewer himself/herself is a member of the group you either hate or pretend to be.

- Invent *a previously unknown minority group** and loudly proclaim its virtues, and how brutally your people have always been victimized.

* E.g., Greco-Sicilian Irish-Canadians; Left Handed Albinos; Unemployed Male Lesbians; Presbyterian Bikers For Buddha; etc.

(7) *Doze Off While the Interviewer Is Speaking.* This rarely fails to interrupt any dialogue that may have been developing between the interviewer and interviewee. If awakened, immediate ask when you can start, what the bonus structure is like, and how many vacation days you can take, effective immediately.

(8) *Soil Yourself and Your Immediate Surroundings.* (See Chapter Two advice on making yourself revolting through *Power Repulsiveness.*)

Failing Interviewers' Screening Questions

Interviewers often try to trick job applicants into revealing inconvenient and maybe dangerous things about themselves. They use sneaky questions written by weasely little people in the Human Resources Department. Don't let the name fool you. "Human Resources" really means just "Employment," or "Hiring Office," but "Human Resources" makes it sound as if the company really thinks that humans are as important to them as, say, coal, molybdenum or other natural elements. It is comforting to some people to realize that, if they go to work for the company, they will be treated with the same respect that management and shareholders have for coal or molybdenum. What is less obvious is that, in the eyes of management and shareholders, they will always be as valuable, and as interchangeable, as chunks of coal or molybdenum. But never *more* valuable than chunks of coal or molybeddenum.

Keep that forever in mind.

Also remember this: anyone with the power to hire you *also has the power to keep you from being hired.* All they need do is not pass your application along to whomever in the company is looking for workers. From the *Loser Aspirant's* point of view – who aspires to *Plummet* – this is good news. Often contact with only one such person can accomplish the failure to be hired.

CASE HISTORY:
Examples Of Losing Interviewee Answers

Following are typical questions asked by *Human Resources* interviewers, with answers that have ensured swift *Plummeting* for "job applicants" whose failures later proved outstanding. You need not memorize the answers word for word, so long as you clearly convey the central ideas.

Q: *How did you learn about this job opening?*

- *I read it on the Men's Room wall at the Greyhound Station. That's where I get all my hot tips.*
- *My cellmate heard about [COMPANY] on the grapevine. We thought that one of us should interview here. I drew the short straw.*
- *Job opening? Job opening? What's this about a job?*

Q: *What are your ambitions?*

- *I'd like to meet some new [babes/studs] for excessive – and preferably noisy – sexual experimentation, preferably on company time.*

- *If everything goes according to plan, I'll have your job in 90 days, maybe 120, and send you packing to the bread lines, Buster.*

- *I'm gonna drain this pop stand dry. After that, I'll have enough cash to run for Congress.*

Q: *What was the reason for your leaving your last job?*

- *Let's just say that the Chairman's son/daughter won't stop smiling for a long, long time!*

- *OK, so the stupid Ethics Committee was in a bad mood. Can we just leave it at that?*

- *Leaving my last job? Wait a second – don't I still work here?*

Q: *Which special talents or abilities qualify you for this position?*

- *Well, I can make myself invisible at will. Also, I know how to walk through walls without breaking the plaster.*

- *The Flax People of Pluto trained me to handle a vast array of commercial situations.*

- *Hey, nobody told me I had to have qualifications for this position!*

It's Never Too Late To Fail !

Even if you're quite sure the interview was the disaster you hoped for, it is wise to give yourself every possible disadvantage. Follow up with a thank you note to the interviewer. This offers the opportunity to drive the final nail in the coffin.

The follow-up letter should include these elements:

1. *Mis-Spelling the Name of the Interviewer You Are Writing to "Thank."*

Most *Human Resources* personnel, even the bad spellers among them, probably can spell their own names. We are emotionally attached to our names, having spent our formative years learning them. People are quite proud of their names. So "name abuse," even accidental, can be jarring. Good! Remember that the more you jar Human Resources interviewers, the less likely they are to validate you for a job.

Obviously, in the best of all possible worlds, the *Failure Aspirant* would also mis-spell the company address on the envelope, thereby failing to send a thank you note at all. Inspired!

2. *Cosmically Inappropriate Personal Comments*

Ask about the health of the interviewer's bowels. If he is satisfying his wife lately, and if so, what proof he has that she isn't faking it – as usual. "Ha ha ha. Just kidding!" Invite him for an intimate getaway weekend on the coast; he may bring his wife also if she's into threesomes. Remember that there are as many offensive comments as pleasant comments – maybe even more – so you have a great deal of opportunity here!

CASE HISTORY:
Sample "Thank You" Note

If the interview was, for example, with a Mr. Claude Simpson of Crown Industries, for a job as a regional sales manager, the *Failure Aspirant* might write the following:

Mr Clod Simpleton

Clown Indistries
[ADDRESS and DATE]

Hi Mr. Sampleson,

I relly liked the interview for the night watchmen job last was it Tuesday? Maybe Wensday? Anyhow. I hope I get the job since I ned to pay some dets, especially the $$$ I owe Big Vito. I like my nees, ha ha ha. How soon can I start, Ms. Slimpsen?

Yours truley,
[YOUR NAME, ALSO MIS-SPELLED]

P.S. Do you still hav that stain on the front of yer pants?

Failing At Keeping A Job You Accidentally Got

Sometimes the abovementioned measures are not quite enough to accomplish failure, and, despite your best efforts, you do get hired. What do you do now?

Problem:

- Despite everything, your new boss seems to appreciate you, and is apparently making efforts to be reasonable, tolerant and helpful. Although you try to be inefficient, work short hours and take forever to accomplish little, he/she remains patient with you. You do your damndest to make sure that the little you do, is very badly done. You even obstruct the work of others, cripppling their efficiency. Still, the boss refuses to recognize your catastrophic lack of ability and motivation. Or if she/he *does* notice it, some inborn sense of decency prevents her/him from acknowledging just how awful you are. Demotion consistently eludes you. At this rate you will *never* be fired. Darn it all. You're reaching the end of your tether. What to do?

Solution:

- As we persist in saying, *persist!* If inefficiency and sloth are not sufficient unto the day, call in reinforcements from other *Failure* categories. The answer may not be as simple as being notoriously inefficient, lazy and obstructionist. You may also need to become *obstreperously surly.* If that combination is not enough to accomplish demotion or dismissal, experiment with *absenteeism,* which often works when applied assiduously enough along with the foregoing. Finally, when and if you *do* show up, remember to be not only lazy, inefficient, obstructionist, obstreperously surly, be sure that your *"low-giene"* is at peak ripeness. Do not bathe or groom yourself, and be sure that you have *dressed for failure!*

Analysis:

- While we do not endorse violence that may cause physical harm or death, *flagrant, noisy aggressive behavior* is always an effective element in the quest for ignominious dismissal. Similarly, although the authors abhor (and never recommend) actual criminal malfeasance, remember that employers are uncomfortable with employees who *frequently allude to a criminal past* or, even more menacing, *a criminal future.*

CASE HISTORY:
Sample Implied Criminality Comments

- *You know, this place would be a cinch to knock over. Even easier than my last heist. Errr ... I mean, "company."*
- *Any idea where they keep the combination to the safe? What kind of security system does it have?*
- *That guy Rob in Accounting looks just like I guy I used to know when I was inside.*
- *This joint isn't big enough to keep* me *down!*
- *I've got me some plans for the future. Yes sir,* big *plans. Just you wait. Just you wait! (Smile as if at some private joke.)*

CHAPTER SEVEN

FAILURE IN ADVERTISING AND MARKETING
by
J. Finley Camerson

J. Finley Camerson drifted into advertising after several previous drifts into Len's Marine Insurance *of Gallup, NM; into managment of the Boise, ID branch of* Kwik-Chee, *a North Korean fast-barbecue franschise; into a brief stint in North Dakota, coaching the* Bismarck "Wisteria" *(Baptist Ladies' Fortnightly Club softball and gardening team); into an even briefer stint in the* U.S. Marines *(he was mustered out shortly after reveille on Day Two "for Convenience of Government); and finally ... into his own short-lived advertising agency, Camerson, Benno, Garuda, Gutiérrez,*

Frankel, Miffler, Marx, Phipps, Another Marx and Chen, of Ballinger, TX.

"My variety of experience had uniquely qualified me for a truly resounding failure in Advertising," he writes, "Since Advertising is a profession that spans virtually all commercial and community entetprises." He is quite correct.

Few other occupations offer such a rich and varied opportunity for Comprehensive Catastrophic Failure *as Advertising. Here are Mr. Camerson's insightful words, written expressly for this volume only days before his removal to what his therapists will only describe as "a much more appropriate environment for Mr. Camerson." – The Editors*

Built-In Failure Opportunities In A Major Industry

There is a huge difference between making advertising and making a living in advertising. It is the difference between theory and reality, not unlike the difference between panting and gasping over centerfold pinups and spending quality time with real women.

If you wish to prosper in the advertising business, it's not enough to have good job skills. You also need a set of personal survival skills. That's because a successful advertising career depends upon a complex series of human interactions, far more than in most other professions. Before your brilliant ad can enthrall the public, it must be filtered through many internal levels, all presided over by ... too many other people. Your career is in their hands. You therefore have to interact with them. The degree to which you interact successfully with them determines how well your career will proceed.

The less successfully you learn to interact, the faster you can expect to *Plummet* to *Super Failure* or better.

So listen up.

The two kinds of people you will deal with are clients and colleagues, ranging from delightful and brilliant to treacherous and unimaginably stupid. Your professional success or failure depends upon how you deal with them. If you play well, you succeed. If not, you fail.

And that's good news!

Although we are rarely in the habit of flaunting our worst qualities, sooner or later they will emerge if given half a chance. We advise giving them at least three-quarters of chance at first – then gradually ratcheting up to 100% of a chance, just so there are no mistakes. There are four cardinal rules of Advertising, which, if violated, guarantee a speedy exit.

Rule #1. Never make anyone think you're either better or worse than they are. Ad agency people are conditioned to feel threatened by (a) your skill – which means you'll have their job by next Tuesday; or (b) your lack of skill – which means they'll be fired by next Tuesday because they were dumb enough to hire you. So you see, in the ad biz you can *Plummet* to *Failure* in both ways!

Rule #2. Adore meetings. They are the main activity in ad agencies. But meetings (with colleagues, clients, outside entities) almost never accomplish anything. Here's your chance to build *Failure!* Learn to make meetings not just passively meaningless, but actively anti-accomplishment. Dramatically unravel anything that may have accidentally been accomplished in earlier meetings.

Rule #3. Play golf. Golf rules the world. That pseudo-sport is so important to any corporate culture that it is in fact the one element that distinguishes the fast-track career from the instant flunk-out. The ability to play – and constantly talk about – golf is what separates the millionaires from the dozenaires. When it is said that "more business is done on the golf course than in the board room," it's absolutely true.

So here's an excellent *Super Failure Hint*: Play golf badly! Become a serial divot producer. Chew up the greens with wild golf-cart driving. Urinate - or worse— in the sandtraps. Play loud rap music (is there any other kind?) on your boom box while others are lining up their putts. Better still, constantly make disparaging jokes about golf and golfers.

Rule #4. Refuse to play the "euphemism game." Advertising is the very *House of Euphemism*. Ignore polite nonsense like "I have a bit of a problem with..." or "Is that headline working hard enough for us?" or "Could work if properly handled."

Instead do the unthinkable, the unforgiveable. *Say what you really mean,* and your pink slip will be streaking toward you before your words have stopped echoing off the mahogany desks and corny fey paintings of English fox hunting scenes: "I can't stand this crap!" "What dickhead wrote this piece of shit?" "This project is doomed to crash and burn!" Or the ultimate deal-breaker: "What is *wrong* with you people anyway?"

What is wrong with them is simple: they chose careers in Advertising. Luckily for you, you have an exit strategy that will work brilliantly if you follow these guidelines.

Good luck!

A Look At Specific Departmental Failure Opportunities

Countless *Loser's Guide* alumni have *Plummeted* to *Catastrophic Comprehensive Failure* via the advertising agency route. Based on the distilled wisdom they have shared with us (see above), the following commentary reveals golden opportunities for Plummeting offered by various job categories in Ad Biz. Mastery of this insider information will help speed *Failure Aspirants* briskly on their way.

Extracted from our *Guest Loser's* recent notes, as clearly as we could decipher his writing, which was done in *Pixie Pink* lipstick on paper towels:

The Creative Department

Creative People are interchangeable, dispensable hacks. Copywriters and Art Directors are loony irresponsible showoffs who want to embarrass the agency and make the client a laughing stock. Their clothes are no damn good. They like to wear beards or handlebar moustaches, especially the men. Their offices are cluttered with cutesy props like barber chairs, old banjos and gas masks. Ha ha ha. They put clever graphics on their walls to show how "creative" they are; but don't be fooled – they – are all burnt-out grinds. Creatives are seditious, drunken punsters who will surely lose the account for us and end up as murderers, suicides or worse.

The Account Group

Account Executives are bootlicking politicos in empty suits with inflated salaries and understaffed imaginations, who exist mainly to play golf and eat costly meals with the client. They write long memos choked with statistics and nonspecific exhortations to do better. They are like used car salesmen who dress well and know when to use the subjunctive mood. Account droids surely coined indispensable Ad Biz phrases like "Could work if properly handled," "Is this okay with Legal?" and "What do you think, Dick?" Because of this intellectual clout, Account People end up with all the top-level jobs, except for one token Executive Creative Director whom they allow on the Executive Committee so they can tell prospective clients that the agency is "really creative."

The Media Department

Media Personnel are number-crunching sluts who read everything out of Meeting Books prepared by researchers. They never smile during conferences. They breakfast, lunch and sup with clients and with hucksters from broadcast and print media who pretend that their medium is the best deal in history for the agency's client. The Media sluts keep right on chewing and pretend to believe this claptrap. It doesn't matter, as long as the meal is paid for by the huckster, which it always is. Unlike Account People, Media folks never buy anything for anyone, not even on their expense account. They also enjoy freebie trips to adorable warm places and try in vain to get laid under the palm fronds. Nobody knows exactly what it is they do for a living, but they are ashamed to admit it.

The Research Department

Research Geeks sit around all day processing mounds of high-brained psycho-babble. They claim to know the exact location of consumers' "hot buttons." When no one is looking they lick their computers. Their bookshelves bulge with volumes with titles like "Grapho-Graphic Sub-Strata Analysis" and "Evaluating Consumer

Paratrends." At night they slip into black hoods, sift through goat entrails and inhale strange fumes. This methodology results in reports that convince the client that the agency's strategy is brilliant and 100% certain to triple his profits by sundown. Research proves that the Creative is wrong, wrong, all wrong. Research people always have pasty flesh and teeny privates and wear undershirts. They grind their teeth in their sleep.

The Production Department

Agency Producers are to commercials what Scotch Tape is to the Space Shuttle. Their job is to remind the client that making commercials is a superhumanly difficult task, never to be entrusted to unshepherded film companies. Producers therefore endure travel, posh hotels, and long, long hours casting for gorgeous actresses who must be, um, validated over dinner. You know, to make sure that the chemistry is, uh, just right. Producers always have their picture taken with the client on the set, often seated together smiling astride a Mitchell crane. They eventually leave the agency to become movie directors because advertising just isn't challenging enough any more.

Finally, A Word About Clients

Clients are arrogant fools without a brain in their heads or the faintest idea of what makes good advertising – or why. They want their company logo larger, ever larger in the ads, much larger. They say things like "Could we lose that humor? There's nothing funny about selling this product, you know!" Clients exist mainly to cause huge running sores in the stomach linings of ad people, and to make sure that the agency wins no Clio Awards. Clients have ugly wives or weasely little husbands, sometimes both. They are much richer than ad people. Clients always beat agency people at golf and everything else, but never ever suspect why.

The more quickly, frequently and profoundly you offend the client, the sooner you are likely to *Power-Fail* – and you will be mere steps away from a spectacular *Plummet!*

Encouragement For Advertising Failure Aspirants

If the above-mentioned Wisdom is properly absorbed, the advertising-based *Failure Aspirant* will have armed himself/herself with important clues to hasten his/her *Plummet* into self-destruction. Unfortunately, there is often unintended competition for your *Failure* ! That's because newcomers usually fail to appreciate that everyone outside their department (and most within their department) is either an actual or a potential enemy, and therefore naively associate with people in disciplines other than their own. Some misguided neophytes stray from the path and actually *cooperate* with colleagues rather than competing with them! Can you imagine? Others are foolish enough to offer assistance – real, not feigned assistance – to their fellows in their agencies' sister offices. Still others commit egregious no-no's like expressing their true opinions, or working overtime without first making sure that the *Executive Committee* is aware of it.

Of course those goofballs are few and far between – and getting even fewer and farther between as the economy shrivels. Usually people who get jobs at ad agencies quickly learn to do everything in their power to keep those jobs, and even to earn promotions! Unlike you, they dread being weeded out and returned to the street, to "the beach" or to the sad grey world of penny journalism.

But your opportunities for *Plummeting* are many, since you are wise enough *not* to hanker for a long, happy, safe career in advertising. *You can easily avoid safety and success because your fate is in your own incompetent hands* – and those of the client. And your bosses. And almost everybody else. So take every chance you get to be incompetent, surly, ill dressed and otherwise offensive [See Above]. Volunteer for everything, especially for projects for which you have no skills, and which do not interest you. Point out the mistakes of your superiors, loudly and publicly, whenever possible. And when they finally get around to firing you, which they certainly will, don't forget to threaten them with major lawsuits.

CHAPTER EIGHT

FAILURE AT HEALTH AND FITNESS

by
J. Bosco Brevoort, M.D.
Senior Illness Fellow
Norfolk Nostril Institute
and
Dick LaJack, Jr.
Personal Trainer to Hollywood Agents

After one fizzled attempt as an undergraduate in Accounting, due to a congenital inability to distinguish among numbers; and another in Classical Languages – he was unskilled in both Latin and Greek – J. Bosco "Jaybee" Brevoort wisely switched to medicine. After graduation from the rigorous course at Nick and Larry's School of Medicine in Bayonne, N.J., he completed a residency in Nasal Medicine *at The Mrs. Gladine Cheeks Memorial Hospital in Fork Junction, NE. Armed with his Board Certification, Jaybee established the prestigious Norfolk Nostril Institute, where he has treated many prominent noses. Winner of the* Philip and Edna O'Connell Medal *for his pioneering work in Corrective Nostrilplasty, Dr. Brevoort has generously consented to co-write this chapter.*

Master Personal Trainer Dick LaJack, Jr. hails from Ballinger, TX. He has simply enormous *arms and a totally "ripped" body. He is much sought after. – The Editors*

Health: An Overrated, Outdated Concept

If you're reading this, it's because you're alive (and you know how to read). But that's just a temporary situation, because guess what? The joke's on you. Eventually you *won't* be able to read this – not because you're likely to forget how to read, but because *you will be dead.* Nothing personal, friend. Please don't consider this a threat. It's just historical fact. As far as we know, everybody who was ever born eventually ended up dying. And you are no exception.

For such a common occurrence, death – although universally acknowledged as the predictable, natural end to life – seems to be a bothersome concept for most people to process. People don't like to have an end date stamped on their lives. They prefer to believe that the best outcome of a life well lived is continue living forever, and failing that, to live as long as possible. They seem to feel that the longer their meaningless, vapid, empty life lasts, the better their chances to win the lottery or finish writing their meaningless, vapid, empty novel. In reality, even if they lived for a thousand years, all most of them would do is sit in the back yard of their suburban Tampa condominium, breathing in and out, in and out, in and out, sucking up their fair share of the planet's dwindling oxygen supply. Then they would go inside to watch meaningless, vapid, empty daytime TV shows, and hobble off at 4:00 P.M. to the nearest *Holiday Inn* or *Cracker Barrel* for the

Early Bird Dinner – Today's Specials!!!

- *Macaroni & Cheese or Chicken Fingers & Fries*
- *Green Salad or Cole Slaw*
- *Choice of Ranch or Italian Dressing*
- *Bread, Bagel or Roll*
- *Iced Tea or Tiny Gulp Soft Drink.*

Tell the truth. Is it really worth living an extra decade or two just to push that kind of abysmal nutritional twaddle through your digestive system?

Indeed, as a *Failure Aspirant*, you are surely wondering: Why would anyone who truly wishes *natural* happiness, wish to fight *Nature's Inevitability*? "It's not nice to fool Mother Nature!"

Let us be clear. The authors emphatically *do not recommend* rushing prematurely into the jaws of *Death*; that is just as unreasonable as artificially prolonging *Life*. Clearly suicide is bratty and thoughtless, and rudely shortcuts *Nature's Inevitability*. It can also be messy, and causes needless unhappiness for innocent people, not to mention lots of paperwork for administrative officials.

Even worse, it deprives us medical professionals of the full measure of years of listening to your chicken-chests, tapping your knobby knees, palpating your distended bellies, prescribing costly drugs with tongue-twister names to calm your hypochondria ... and sending bills that – assuming you can pay them – enable us to carpet our summer homes and join classier country clubs.

Fitness: Another Hoax Exposed

Countless millions struggle vainly not only to stay young, but to reverse the aging process, frantically stiff-arming the *Grim Reaper* with exercise and nutritional supplements; visits to health care practicioners and sleek cosmetic surgeons; and in a slightly different context, constantly quashing the temptation to fondle Big Nunzio's kid sister.

They do all this, and more, in the name of something trendily called "staying fit."

As stated above, we object to suicide. But that doesn't mean that those aspiring to *Health Failure* can't help *Mother Nature* lead you to the quickest possible natural demise. There's no rule that says you have to take unreasonably good care of yourselves.

Therefore, joyously embrace the glorious alternative: Become fanatically opposed to zealously healthy behavior. Our advice to you:

- Eat what you please, when you please, as often as possible.
- Get little or no rest – relaxation is a cruel myth designed to lead to unnecessary comfort and ease.

- Strenuously avoid exercise. It just jiggles odd-shaped internal organs and dampens your armpits.
- Ignore all that mumbo-jumbo "advice from fitness experts."

CHAPTER NINE

FAILURE AT SCIENCE AND TECHNOLOGY
by
Leander Trillup, Ph.D., M.D.
and
Quasimodo L. Zep, E.E., D.V.M., R.N.

Doctor Trillup received his doctorate in Vertebrate Philosophy from Samoa Open University with his groundbreaking dissertation, Spines and the Thought Process. *After taking an M.D. at Kyrgyzstan Argicultural & Equestrian College, he returned to his native Scotland to run his family's haggis factory. At this writing he has run it nearly into the ground.*

Mr. Zep knows a lot about electricity, especially as it applies to veterinarian electroshock therapy. His nursing background has equipped him to keep careful records of his patients' vital signs, some more vital than others. He is fairly tall. At this writing, Mr. Zep was recovering from a persistent dry cough. – The Editors

Science And Technology: Religions Of Modern Man

Among society's most admired citizens are those who show their brilliance by succeeding at *Science* and *Technology*. Scientists and technologists invent computer systems that make them overnight quadrillionaires. They develop medical processes that bring back entire nations from the dead. They track down species long believed extinct. They show us clever ways to whistle with a mouth full of sauerkraut, never once missing a note. They qualify for car loans.

Being famous and rich – the two main determinants of "success" in modern society – they are natural role models for teenage slackers hunched over hand-held entertainment units, awaiting an uncertain future.

It is almost always hard to prove that you have succeeded in the arts, or in social sciences, since accomplishment in those fields is largely subjective. But success in objective "hard sciences" and technology is unmistakable due to the irrefutable fact of physical proof. No mere opinions can interfere with real-world evidence. No amount of viewpoint, taste considerations, inspiration or emotional content can change the facts: the bridge stayed up. The rocket landed on Mars. The bank account *did* balance. The computer printed out the page. Alexander Graham Bell really did say "Mr. Watson, come here – I want to see you!" And Mr. Watson really did hear that first telephone call. Numbers add up; engines behave properly; hacking coughs are cured. That new planet shows up exactly where and when it was predicted.

Result: scientists and technologists receive Nobel Prizes from somber Scandinavian men in dignified suits, some lightly flecked with herring.

It is hard to imagine any more dramatic example of "success" than doing well in science and technology.

This is more good news for the science-based *Failure Aspirant!* To *Plummet* from such a prestigious, dizzying height is all the more thrilling: so definitively catastrophic; so deliciously humiliating! All one needs to do is to establish up a "serious scientific" platform, then tumble dramatically from it, to the scorn and derision of one's peers.

CASE HISTORY:
Propositions That Shook The Scientific World – With Laughter !

Q: Who among us would be bold enough to challenge confident, formula-packed statements such as these?
A: Anyone with basic understanding of mathematics and physics.

The following are excerpted from monographs delivered – by several of our *Super Failure* alumni – to open-mouthed audiences at prestigious scientific congresses:

- *... and so, it is all too obvious that* $5x + \Updownarrow (45/\bar{\lambda}) + (\beta 5\mu) = \triangleright$, *notwithstanding the Discursive Fractal Flumerant* $(\bar{\lambda}/3m\exists 66) - (7.\subseteq + \Psi/\sqrt{-1})(/5) + \notin = \Re(!)$, *despite Mandelbrot's insistence to the contrary. But then, he was an angry, dyspeptic little man. Why, Fermat and Euler each, from his own separate griffpoint, discrealed Poincaré's naive assertion that* $(44x/\infty)$ *at value* $\theta/\Im$, *reduced by* $4(9n-\Omega)$,*could not approach the sectioned* $(\forall\uparrow\Sigma)$ *Deppel Point unimpeded by* $[(4\eta+(\exists\downarrow\Sigma) + (-1)]$ *as we have previously so brilliantly demonstrated* (Weaselton, Gripfelder, Bong, Tifflock, 1998c).

- *Therefore, murdling the Klarfelder Elements* $(5g+\Gamma^{\circ} + 6\Xi) + (\chi 4\varpi)$, *having undulated the Carmody-Zick Obversification* $(2\lozenge\ldots\ 1\lozenge\ldots\ \hookleftarrow\ldots\ !)$, *we are left with the starkly unavoidable conclusion that* $q/Q = (3 \Leftrightarrow 3/) \ldots (\chi\Delta\pi\Psi)$*, which gives us* $E=mc^{TM}$*. Or, in layman's terms, the ferry will surely sink with that many Bangladeshis on board.*

- *Updating the Nilssworth Trajectory, Duckwad and Blibber postulated that* $(d \leftrightarrow d) + (\leftrightarrow \mu\phi\perp$ *value* $\Delta 7 \Diamond)$ *could result only in* $[(*\nabla) + (d \leftrightarrow d)\pm^{\circ}]$ *(!) where* $\Pi \rightarrow \zeta$ *and* $\zeta < \subseteq$*. The two trains would therefore not meet. At least, not on time.*

- *... which puts us in mind of the Classical Logic question, popularly known as "Lenny's Paradox": Hank is shorter than Gladys; Roberto is twice as wide as Helena (who is taller than Hank but not as narrow as Gladys); Gioacchino has red hair; Helena's hair is narrower and redder than Roberto's hair; and all are standing on a platform 30cm above level ground. Are the following statements True, False or Undeterminable?*

  1. *Helena is dating Hank.*
  2. *Hank's parents approve; Helena's parents think he is too short for her.*
  3. *Norm does not appear in the above equation. He's with Lenny.*
  4. *Red hair is harder to maintain than brown hair.*

CASE HISTORY:
Biological Conundrums

The biological sciences, also, have their glittering moments, which can be twisted to our advantage. For example:

- *Phylogeny recapitulates ontongeny – but what does it do for an encore?*

- *Evolution combines DNA variations, resulting in the continuation of the fittest species. This is often the DNA with the biggest knockers.*

- *Nature abhors a vacuum. A vacuum can't stand Nature either, so they're even.*

- *Mighty oaks from tiny acorns grow. Then they are cut down to make space for shopping malls.*

- *The left brain controls rational thought. The right brain controls emotion and artistic abstractions. Interestingly, both sides of the brain are equally wrinkly and gooey.*

CHAPTER TEN

FAILURE AT SPORTS AND MARTIAL ARTS

by
Coach Biff R. "Yip" Stiffner
and
Hon. Yakuza She-Dong
21st Degree Chop Wak Master

Indiana-born Biff R. "Yip" Stiffner spent his boyhood as a "military brat" in far-flung postings such as Guam, Bhutan, Lapland, Laos and other exotic locales. This gave him extensive exposure to sports unknown to most

Americans. As one of only three Indianapolis teenagers skilled at Aztec skull-tossing games, he quickly became captain of his high school's Tlachtli team. Following that early success, he tried to interest the school district in other sports he had mastered during his wandering childhood years. Yet he failed to introduce Indiana to Underwater Hockey, Blindfold Jousting, Cheese Rolling, Bog Snorkeling, Dwarf Tossing, Wife Carrying and Tag-Team Bungee Jumping. After earning his Master's Degree in Sports and Recreation from the University of Ulan Bator, he returned to America to coach "normal American" sports at high schools in and around Indianapolis. He claims not to be bitter.

The Honorable Yakuza She-Dong is tall for an Okinawan of Chinese descent. He is tall for almost any nationality, although his exact height is a closely-guarded secret by the country in whose intelligence community he serves. Mr. Yakuza is unrelated to the dreaded Japanese mafia that bears the same name – it is just an unfortunate coincidence. It is rumored that he is the Director of Self-Defense and Close Combat Training for Norway's commando forces. Oslo will neither confirm nor deny this, but can it be another mere coincidence that Mr. Yakuza's favorite food is Herring Sushi? – The Editors

---

Sports Need Not Be Fun

If there is one thing of universal interest to men and women all over the planet, that one thing is surely sports. Nearly every stable society in the world has devoted individuals and teams participating regularly in casual or organized sports. Industrialized countries have fattened their broadcast schedules to cover more sports than ever before, more regularly than ever before and for longer seasons than ever before.

Given the constantly-improving skills exhibited by athletes of every kind, all over the world, record performances are being posted with increasing frequency. Some world records last only a matter of months or even weeks. It is not unheard-of for a new world record to be set, only to be bettered (sometimes by the same athlete) with hours or days.

The ruthless American attitude, “Winning isn’t the best thing – it’s the *only* thing,” teaches children that second place is the sporting equivalent of rancid chopped liver or moldy peanut butter. “You don’t win the silver – you lose the gold, you mealy-mouthed, panty-waist, repulsive little loser!” shriek battalions of downhearted parents when little Cooter Bob or Dolores Jane don’t live up to World Class standards in the elementary school sports day.

Forget Grantland Rice’s naive, treacly observation!

For when the One Great Scorer comes
To write against your name,
He marks – not that you won or lost –
But how you played the game.

What did a mere sports journalist know about the joys of *Catastrophic Comprehensive Failure;* the unearthly happiness of being last in the Marathon; blowing a 9" putt; muffing the pop-up or slow grounder that would have been the final out; being brutally KO'd at :29 of the first round? Could a famous sportswriter, accustomed to the drama of sportsmen giving *Their All,* possibly understand the subtlety of F*ailure Aspirants* whose undying motivation is to give *Their Nothing?*

Baseball:

- Remember that umpires are human, and as such are prone to error. It is greatly amusing to keep reminding them of this. Cultivation of this habit will have a direct effect on your career!

- Never interrupt the path of a grounder or a line drive. Clearly the ball is just following the trajectory that physics has intended for it, and to interrupt that path is to be disrespectful of the Natural Order. It is bad karma.

- Be innovative. Try pitching to left field instead of to the plate. When you hit the ball safely, run to third base instead of to first. If you get a base on balls, refuse to take first base, and retire instead to the dugout to catch up on your reading.

- Be the tenth player on the field whenever possible; it refreshes the umpires' minds and provides an entertaining interlude for the fans. See if you can convince teammates to join you.

Football:

- Refuse to wear a helmet. If you wanted to be treated gently you would have joined the chess club instead of the football team.

- Experiment with *New Directions in Uniforms.* Any fool can dress exactly like the other members of the team. The bold *Failure Aspirant* will instead match his wardrobe to the cheerleaders, hot dog vendors or some favorite fictional Super Hero.

- As you line up for play, loudly inform the opposing players who will be carrying the ball for your team, and where. This will "level the playing field," and enhance your chances of landing a starting position on the other team. They probably have nicer players anyway.

Soccer:

- There is no such thing as soccer. It is a worldwide conspiracy, an illusion designed expressly to make Americans reject Underwater Hockey, Blindfold Jousting, Cheese Rolling, Bog Snorkeling, Dwarf Tossing, Wife Carrying and Tag-Team Bungee Jumping. Now *those* are sports worth playing.

Basketball:

- Try to be extremely tall, graceful and preferably of African descent. If you can not accomplish these three objectives, strive to be as pale, dwarfish and uncoordinated as possible. This will earn much sympathy from spectators, and make much more comfortable with your inevitable lopsided defeats.

CASE HISTORY:
Example Of A Faux-Sports "Sport"

The Americas Cup yacht race is surely the most mind-bogglingly useless "sports" event in history. It's a super elitist "sport" that virtually nobody on earth ever gets to play. By comparison, even the staggeringly hypocritical Olympic Games seem noble and useful, and golf "classics" appear democratic and populist. The "A-Cup" pits the priceless yachts of elitist zillionaire WASPs from some English-speaking countries against the priceless yachts of elitist zillionaire WASPs of *other* English-speaking countries to determine which elitist zillionaire WASPs get to keep a gaudy metal trophy in their gaudy home marina for two years. Will our WASPs whip their WASPs? If not, whose WASPs will our walloping WASPs whip? The suspense is ... very nearly unbearable, darling.

Forget everything you have seen in action movies, or taped/DVD courses on self-defense. It's just show business glitz – flailing and spinning; striking and kicking; ducking and blocking – pure fiction! It never works in the real world, where (for example) a *Glock 19* semi-automatic pistol with a 15-round magazine of hollow-point 9mm parabellum downloads far more kinetic energy than any kickboxer's foot. And much faster, too! Face facts: can any amount of training really prepare *you* to move at 1,200 feet per second? We thought not.

That said, the martial arts scream remains a deeply satisfying option. Often, if your lungs are powerful enough, you need not even draw your sidearm.

A refreshing change from the *Glock* can be provided by almost any low-octane flame thrower or rocket propelled grenade launcher (RPGL). Here the main problem is concealment. But when walking through dangerous low income neighborhoods, it is usually advantageous to prominently display your flame thrower or RPGL. Deterrence is a form of victory.

Those aspiring to *Martial Arts Failure* can simply drop their *Glocks* or other fine weapons and (a) try to run or (b) surrender, throwing yourself upon the mercy of dreadful people. They will certainly guarantee your *Super Failure.*

CHAPTER ELEVEN

FAILURE AT ENTERTAINING AND POLITICAL CORRECTNESS

by
Elsa Ffitch-Witherington-Taroo
Society Authority
and
Ahmed M. Jefferson-Arbenz, Ph.D.
Director
Intolerance International

Ms. Ffitch-Witherington-Taroo, of the Luton-Dunstable Ffitch-Witherington-Taroos, has been in simply all the society pages, darlings. And for good reason. She is social. She is universally admired for staging absolutely the chic-est, most sought-after, "A-Plus List" dinner parties, high teas and snacks. Her much-quoted book, Prepare Like The Very Devil; Sup Like An Absolute Angel *is currently in its 13th printing, in its 13th different language. Elsa Ffitch-Witherington-Taroo, initially a raw foods advocate, has finally bought an oven and a stovetop, and uses them to delightful advantage.*

Dr. Jeff-Arb, as familiars call him, has consistently raised hackles while raising social consciousness with his controversial books: Women and Minorities – Must We?; Profiles In Rudeness; *and* Tell It Like It Isn't. *As the Dean of* Eddie's School of Social Work, *he has worked tirelessly for decades to refine techniques for creating more "honest conflict" and less "sappy tolerance for people who aren't as good as we are." He describes his educational mission as "Slapping people awake, the silly geese. Don't they know what's what any more? Damn them anyway." – The Editors*

Failure As A Fancy Dinner Host/Hostess

For centuries, the *Dinner Party* has been perhaps the greatest single element in building social success. Good reputations have been made on a single fabulous dinner party, with the right foods and the right wines served the right way to The Right People. Obviously the reverse is equally true. This gives the *Failure Aspirant* an excellent opportunity to *Plummet* – possibly in a single evening!

[See Chapter Two, ***At The Dinner Table,*** *for additional recommendations. – The Editors]*

Well begun, half done. Remember always to seat people next to those they dislike intensely. This adds an exquisite tension to the occasion, which should always be as strained and sternly formal as possible – in other words, appropriately "high society."

Seating examples:

- Place a wife next to the woman everybody recognizes as the girl friend of her husband.
- If a guest is known for frequent projectile vomiting, make sure he/she sits near the center of the table.
- Seat a Vegan right in front of the roast, and invite him/her to do the carving.
- Make certain that unwashed homeless guests are included, and partnered with the best-dressed fashionistas in the room.
- If there are any clergy present, flank them with aggressively vocal, heavy-drinking atheists. The ministers will surely welcome the challenge of making new converts.

It is essential to present the most preposterously esoteric menu, featuring fashionably obscure foods that real people would ever choose to eat – foods your guests have probably never heard of. No matter. They will later boast of the extravagant delicacies your chef created expressly for your table. No matter how ludicrous and "precious" the dinner you serve, it will be considered a "gourmet triumph" if enough A-Plus List celebrities are present, pretending to enjoy the food.

If you do this right, none of those present will ever again accept your dinner invitation. The following menu spelled the end to the hostess's dreams of a future in polite society. It was reported that most of the guests, upon leaving the dinner, converged upon a local diner and gorged themselves on Lenny's Greaseburger Specials – including Mega-Lard Fries, Deep Fried Suet, Beer Battered Onion Rings and Choice of Hi-Caf Coffee or Painfully Sugary Soft Drink ("Glutton Gulp"). Two were hospitalized but later recovered.

CASE HISTORY:
Sample Preciously Presumptuous Menu

Appetizers

- *Mini-Fillets of Unborn Musk Ox, marinated in Château Haut-Brion 1947, rolled in Pumpernickel*

Crumbs and lightly dusted with Essence of Goat Cheese.

- *Roasted Serbian Eggplant Sections, embedded in Finnish Frog Liver Pâté, glazed with Dundee Marmelade and drizzled with a broth of Garlic Mincemeat.*

- *Chopped Walnut and Giant Walnut Salad on a bed of Steamed Romaine Spears, Braised Quail's Wings, Red Currant Jelly, and Kosher Dill Pickle Caponata, coquettishly splashed with a blend of chilled Chablis and Gatorade.*

Soup

- *Cold Creamed Moose Nose Consommé, relieved by islands of Hot Goat Cheese and Lukewarm Loganberry Stew au Gratin.*

- *Hot Creamed Moose Nose Consommé, relieved by islands of Cold Goat Cheese and Roasted Serbian Eggplant Sections (see above).*

Fish

- *Whole Fresh Hudson River Crappie, sautéed while it swims, served astride a mound of Coconut*

Custard, garnished with Heinz Catsup and Philadelphia Brand Goat Cheese, and topped with a single rum-soaked Iranian Marascino Raisin. (Pond Scum Sauce optional.)

Meat

- *Standing Crotch Roast of Doubly-Aged Veal au Jus, served on Giant Southwest Blue Corn Husk Tortilla, surrounded by Swiss Milk Chocolate Pan Potatoes with chunks of steaming Red Currant Goat Cheese, and crowned with an individual Gâteau de Foie Gras. (Kim Chee is optional.)*

Salad

- *Potpourri Bowl of Tristan da Cunha Tussock Grass, Radicchio, Young Oak Leaves, Privet Hedge Buds, Walnuts with Giant Walnuts, Serbian Goat Cheese, Croatian Goat Cheese, Red Currants, Pink Currants, Pale Cerise Currants, Medium Albany Walnuts with Small Poughkeepsie Walnuts, Lamb Cheese, Arugula, Beef Cheese, Rocky Mountain Dahl Sheep Cheese, and more Radicchio.*

- *Choice of dressings: Butterscotch, Dietetic Muriatic Acid or Blue Goat Cheese.*

Plateau de Fromages

- *Aged Helsinki Velveeta*
- *Icelandic Cod Cheese*
- *Soft Patagonian Wormy Goat.*

Dessert

- *Fluffy Lemon Goat Cheese Cake, marinated in Red Currant Linament, sprayed with Lamb and Atlantic Salmon Steam, drizzled with icy Budweiser Beer, and anointed with an individual skinned Watermelon, poached in Moose Nose Consommé (see above) and drowned in Redi-Whip ®.*

CHAPTER TWELVE

FAILURE AT ADMINISTRATIVE AND LEGAL MATTERS

by

F. Crift Legalson

In order to please his overbearing and embarrassingly wealthy parents, F. Crift Legalson took a law degree from The Mrs. Bessie N. Fletcher School of Law (Distance Learning Program). The School quickly made him give the degree back, for reasons left unexplained. Undeterred, Mr. Legalson established a small legal practice that became gradually smaller. Eventually his practice became limited to one client – Mr. Legalson himself, defending against a series of high profile legal malpractice suits, which became gradually lower profile until they disappeared altogether.

A failed run for Attorney General of his home state (identity of that State withheld at request of its Governor) led to a subsequent run for the somewhat lesser office of Paralegal General. Although he lost that race as well, and by a somewhat larger margin, Mr. Legalson wrote extensively of his legal and political memoirs. The following pages are a distillation of the wisdom he accumulated in his brief yet inconsequential career. Mr. Legalson is married but not entirely sure why. – The Editors

---

So much of our time is spent dealing with *Officialdom* in all its forms, that it behooves the *Failure Aspirant* to learn how best to fail in this crucial and widespread category of social activity. To *Plummet* in legal, civic and other administrative matters is to take a giant step toward *Comprehensive Catastrophic Failure* !

When you deal with anyone representing *Officialdom,* you are perforce dealing with individuals who have the Power, Legal Authority (and usually the Burning Desire!) to make your life truly miserable. Indeed, the more miserable they can make your life, the more fulfilled they feel, professionally and personally. Here this author can speak with some authority, having fulfilled the professional and personal lives of many Official individuals.

Functionaries in many categories are empowered to deprive you of money (fines, penalties, assessments); of your property (car, boat, home or anything else they "levy") – they can even take away your freedom and confine you (for terms up to and including several lifetimes) to unattractive structures where you will rarely find friends who share your interests.

The central reality of these powerful *Officials* is that they are entirely humorless. They take their work, and above all, they take themselves, very seriously. Their merest activity. in their eyes, bears the civic, legal and moral weight of the Holy Grail Itself.

It is helpful to know this because now you already know a quick path to Failure when dealing with these men and women.

- Because they have no trace of humor in their lives, be as humorous as possible (preferably deprecatingly, and always at their expense). Since they will never "get it," their only recourse will be to get you!

- Because they take themselves and their petty functions so seriously, you must take them lightly, scoffing and sniffing at the petty little fluffiness upon which they depend for their self-esteem.

Here the *Failure Apspirant* can easily use to his/her benefit, any skills learned in earlier chapters, including (but not limited to) *Power Repulsiveness*. These are extremely transferable skills.

CASE HISTORY:
Sample Comments To Infuriate Selected Officials

Traffic Policeman:

- *You call that speeding? Piffle! You ain't seen nothing yet!*
- *Weapons in my car? Including chemical or biological agents?*
- *No, I haven't been drinking this evening! I'm still burning off this morning's snootful.*

Internal Revenue Auditor:

- *What'll it take for you to give me a pass on all this?*

- *Whaddya mean, I can't declare Belgium as a dependent?*
- *If you're nice to me, I can get you a job at H&R Block.*

Courtroom Judge:

- *Your Honor, you look like a Sicilian widow in those black duds!*
- *I'll double the other side's offer.*
- *Did your robe come with matching towels?*

Special Case History Section:
Immigration and Customs Inspectors

In every country in the world, Immigration and Customs Inspectors are the least humorous, most self-important and most prickly of all governmental functionaries. As human beings, they are universally less imaginative, skilled or charming than Xerox Room interns at the *Turkish Ministry of Cement*. It is hard to imagine what their job interviews must be like. ("Are your eyes currently open?" "Yes." "Have you breathed recently?" "Yes." "When can you start?")

Here are things to say to these dreadful people that will virtually guarantee keeping you from entering (or maybe leaving) the following countries:

United States of America:

- *Who do I see for my cavity search?*
- *Oh nuts – I forgot to pack all those Iranian cigars.*
- *Is that thing loaded? Can I try it?*

France:

- *Voulez-vous masser mon zizi?*
- *Do we have to declare English wines and cheese?*
- *Frankly, I never much cared for Edith Piaf.*

England:

- *Sorry, I can't recall exactly who packed my bags.*
- *Can you keep a secret? My real name is Ahmed!*
- *How come nobody ever tips over those rocks at Stonehenge?*

Canada:

- *So – you're still wearing those corny old Sam Browne belts!*

- *No idea how long we'll be in Canada – probably just long enough to knock off a convenience store or two.*
- *Hey, is it true you guys are planning to make this place our 51st State?*

Russia:

- *Pssst! Could you use a couple pairs of Levis?*
- *Hi, Boris. Where can I score some really old icons?*
- *I hear that Tolstoy's novels were really written by Christopher Marlowe.*

Extra Special Case History Section: Food and Beverage Inspectors

Everybody, whether they wish to succeed or to fail, needs to eat. If you starve to death, you can clearly claim *Comprehensive Catastrophic Failure* in the categories *Health and Nutrition* and *Staying Alive.* But you would equally clearly have succeeded in the category *Starving to Death.*

Anyone who needs to eat, usually prefers to eat food. Since food is of such importance, it is carefully monitored for cleanliness, nutritional value and general safety by government agencies and sometimes even religious entitites. Food inspectors have the power to condemn your food. This means they can put your restaurant, pushcart, ranch or meat packing plant out of business.

Seen in a more positive light, a food inspector can be a great ally in your quest for *Failure*. But you can help yourself even more with comments like these:

- *Roaches in our sausage meat? Aw, shucks, Inspector – protein is protein, right?*
- *We just expanded our packing operation into the men's room. The ladies' room was too untidy.*
- *Behind this door is our Fish Recycling Department. Want a mint?*
- *We get much faster production if workers don't have to keep stopping to wash their hands.*
- *We change aprons and hair nets every day – from one worker to another. Cuts our laundry bills way down!*
- *We always slip some rat poison into the pasta sauce. I mean – who wants rats in their sauce?*

- *And under these decomposing potatoes ... I think you'll find an envelope you're* really gonna like!

CHAPTER THIRTEEN

FAILURE AT BEAUTY AND FASHION
by
Carmelita von Lippenstift
and
Yves Du Drageur

[NOTE: This chapter has been expunged by the Editors as totally redundant. Everything you need to know about Failure at Beauty and Fashion *has already been explained, one way or another, in preceding chapters. Besides that, by eliminating these pages, the contributing Guest Losers can claim yet another – if totally unexpected* – Failure*: the* Failure to Have a Chapter on Failure at Beauty and Fashion *published. Bravi! – The Editors]*

EPILOGUE

The Ultimate Step: Failing At Failure Itself

Gentle Reader, we have spent many pages together, examining the bracingly cold reality of the importance of *Failure* as the essential guiding principle of an ultimately satisfying life. Reverse satisfaction is worth striving for. It can not be stressed too often or too strongly: unless and until we learn joyously to embrace failure and *Plummet*, we will remain in tragic denial of life's ultimate happiness.

But here – in these final pages – we face an interesting paradox.

If *Failure* is the state to which we aspire, the condition upon which our truest happiness and fulfillment depends; and if we manage finally to *Succeed at Failure* – does that success not put us back where we started, in the darkness of a mistaken goal?

Indeed it does. Because if, as we have learned, *Failure* and disappointment and loss is *Nature's Plan* for us, but we have succeeded at *Failure*, then we have in fact lost everything. Until we learn to *Fail at Failure Itself* we can never completely enter the realm of circularity – the ineffable Zen state of failing at everything, including *Failure.*

Hey – maybe you didn't need to buy this book.

Come to think of it, maybe we didn't even need to write it.

Whatever.

A FINAL WORD

Plummet!

ABOUT THE AUTHOR

Before joining the dazzling roster of *Magic Lamp Press* authors, Dean Christopher spent several decades in journalism, advertising and playing jazz piano into the wee hours for sallow-complexioned people with no place to go in the morning. He was never a failure at any of those endeavors, although ad agencies did seem to enjoy firing him for telling unwelcome truths.

His writing has appeared in many magazines, including *National Lampoon, OMNI, SPIN* (a contributing editor for 8 years) and *Discover*, for whom he recently wrote book reviews, articles and a popular book called *Twenty Things You Didn't Know About Everything* (HarperCollins, 2008).

Educated at Georgetown University, the University of Madrid and the Monterey Institute of Foreign Studies, Dean is a committed internationalist.

Before stumbling down the rabbit hole into journalism and marketing, he spent 8 years in the music business in New York and Europe. Besides English, he is fluent in Spanish and French; comfortable in Brazilian Portuguese and Italian; and even has some rudimentary Persian. His German is really awful, but it amuses German people, who laugh and buy him beer.

Dean disclaims any responsibility for the 1883 explosion of the island of Krakatoa. "I was nowhere near the place," he insists – adding that the event happened before his grandparents were born. During his years in Army Intelligence, Dean helped humiliate the International Communist Conspiracy, which has never recovered its self-esteem.

He does not wear a beard, lives frugally in Beverly Hills, California and is clean in thought and deed.

WHAT THE READERS SAY

- The Loser's Guide To Personal Failure *is a breath of searing, realistic air. It takes unerring aim at the ill-defined and illusory notion of "success," demolishing the myth that links it to "happiness" – another outdated concept that the world is far better off without. In these pages, with eyes newly opened, the reader will gasp over the cumulative wisdom of bold losers who have preceded them – those pioneers of Failure, the Super Losers who have brilliantly succeeded in* ***"... milking a grisly, often fibrillating defeat from the honeyed paws of success,"*** *as* The Failed Metaphorist *noted in his highly unsuccessful book* Shall I Compare Thee to Whatever? *which has been out of print for decades.* – The Marginalist Monthly

- *It was never easy talking to the women I met. Now – thanks to the inspiration provided by this book – I've stopped even trying to meet them at all. I spend all day watching* The Loser's Channel. *What a relief!* – Bob "Big Bob" Mc L., Moultrie, GA

- The Loser's Guide *is a welcome antidote to those saccharine, pollyannish "self-help" books that cynically promise the reader "improvement" – as if unevolved creeps (like the present readers) could possibly accomplish by themselves what they were incapable of doing even with professional help! Hah!* – L'Osservatore Romano

- *After I read* The Guide *and realized I was never going to do well with interpersonal relations, I focused all my attention on my career. I got elected to the U.S. Senate! Haven't done well there, either.* – Initials, state and party affiliation withheld upon request

- *I was sad when Big Ernesto left. I cried and cried. Oh how I wept. Then I read* The Loser's Guide. *After that, I knew what to expect from men. They are all simply awful. So I was thrilled last Thursday when Max left. I even laughed, though he was lots nicer than Big Ernesto. Thanks for your help.* – Aquamarine K., Vinita, OK

COMING SOON TO A PAGE NEAR YOU

Look for these blockbuster best sellers
from the pen of Dean Christopher!

- *Bring Shame to Your Village – 10 Easy Lessons or Five Hard Ones*
- *Dean Christopher: The Unauthorized Autobiography*
- *Captured Nazi Parade Plans: Secret Halftime Shows of the Third Reich*
- *It Came From Beneath Second Base: Occult Horror on the Baseball Diamond*

Editor's Note:

For details of books by Dean Christopher, please visit the website
www.DeanChristopher.biz

www.ingramcontent.com/pod-product-compliance
Lightning Source LLC
LaVergne TN
LVHW010055110826
845155LV00028B/346

* 9 7 8 1 8 8 2 6 2 9 9 3 0 *